W9-BFA-202

A Garden Story

A Garden Story

Leon Whiteson

Mercury House
San Francisco

Copyright © 1995 by Leon Whiteson

Published in the United States of America by Mercury House, San Francisco, California, a nonprofit publishing company devoted to the free exchange of ideas and guided by a dedication to literary values.

Originally published by Faber and Faber, Inc., and reprinted by permission.

All rights reserved. No part of this book may be reproduced in any form without permission in writing from the publisher, except by a reviewer who may quote brief passages in a review.

United States Constitution, First Amendment: Congress shall make no law respecting an establishment of religion, or prohibiting the free exercise thereof; or abridging the freedom of speech, or of the press; or the right of the people peaceably to assemble, and to petition the Government for a redress of grievances.

Cover design by Mary Maurer. Cover photographs by Steve Nilsson. Manufactured in the United States of America.

Library of Congress Cataloguing-in-Publication Data:
Whiteson, Leon
    A garden story / Leon Whiteson
      p. cm.
    Originally published: Boston : Faber and Faber, 1995.
    ISBN: 0-56279-089-7 (pbk. : alk. paper)
    1. Gardening—California—Los Angeles. 2. Gardens—California—Los Angeles. 3. Whiteson, Leon. 4. Whiteson, Leon—Homes and haunts—California—Los Angeles. 6. Hollywood (Los Angeles, Calif.)
    I. Title.
[SB455.W524 1996]   96-33311
818'.5403—dc20   CIP

9 8 7 6 5 4 3 2 1
FIRST MERCURY HOUSE EDITION

For Aviva

Contents

1 Dreaming of You *3*

2 Countries of the Mind *17*

3 Opening Chapters *33*

4 Defending Boundaries *51*

5 Zones, Leaves, and Water *71*

6 Listen and Learn *91*

7 Fungus, Rot, and Mildew *107*

8 Restorations *129*

9 Tumult and Tranquillity *147*

A Garden Story

1

Dreaming of You

The garden I made in my Hollywood yard was my first foray into horticulture. When I began it, I was quite innocent of garden lore and totally without practical experience.

In truth, I'd never really wanted to be a gardener. I had a typical writer's preference for working with my head rather than my hands; words and ideas excited my interest, not plants and soils. All the countries I'd lived in before arriving in Los Angeles— Zimbabwe, South Africa, England, Spain, Greece, and Canada—were, to me, essentially landscapes of the mind. Vivid landscapes to be sure, often charged with emotion, but never to be considered as grounds I might directly dig into and cultivate.

My lack of interest in gardening was reinforced by the condition of the house my wife, Aviva, and I bought in the western section of Hollywood in the summer of 1987. The yards, front and back, were desolate. The property had been rented out for years, and it seemed that neither the various tenants nor the absentee owners had ever lavished any tender loving care on the garden. In Los Angeles's dry climate, where constant watering is crucial, the grounds had been left to desiccate.

The front yard featured a plum tree badly in need of pruning and two unkempt bird-of-paradise bushes. A scruffy bank of pines screened the north front property line, and overgrown jade plant bushes ran along the southern line. The backyard was even less attractive. It had a long-dead lawn dominated by a huge avocado tree whose fruit was as wooden as its bark. A ratty banana palm overhung the narrow deck attached to the back bedrooms. Orange and lemon trees, overgrown and semisterile, were tangled up with an old, spider-ridden grapevine that threatened to strangle them to death. A dusty cypress or two completed this sad scene.

The neglected condition of the grounds didn't really bother me. Ever since I was a young architect working in London with Englishmen who went on and on about their tea roses and their "mums," I'd dismissed garden chatter as supremely silly. The notion of horticulture as a hobby struck me as trivial, a pastime for people whose sex lives must be sad.

Our first intervention in the Hollywood backyard was designed simply to increase privacy and security; we hired a contractor to erect an eight-foot timber lattice fence to divide the garden from the small guest house at the rear of the property. In effect, and without quite meaning to, we created a walled enclosure circled by the lattice, and by the back and side fences between our yard and the neighbors'. We paid a gardener to plant a row of bougainvillea vines along the lattice and the fences; bougainvillea grows quickly and demands little attention, and that suited me fine.

A morning glory vine, rooted in a neighbor's yard, sent its tendrils toward one stretch of lattice, adding its bright blue flowers to the garden's southern horizon. The morning glory and the bougainvillea gave me pleasure, reminding me of Spain and Greece, countries I'd lived in for long periods. But at the time I was preoccupied with my job as the staff architecture critic for the Los Angeles *Herald-Examiner* and with the writing of novel titled *Dreaming of You*, set on a remote Greek island.

I began the early chapters of *Dreaming of You* as the October heat began to cool into the breezes of November. On my desk were two stacks of paper. The smaller stack was filled with words; the far larger stack was blank. Slowly, sheet by sheet, paper moved from one pile to the other, through the roller of my IBM Selectric.

Lifting my eyes from the typewriter, I'd see not the dusty Hollywood yard beyond my window, but the vivid presence of the village of Molyvos, on the island of Lesbos in the northeastern Aegean—the setting for my novel. Molyvos, where I settled for four years in the early 1970s, is barely six miles from the Turkish coast and the massive blue mountain ranges of Asia Minor. A ruined Venetian castle tips its crest like an erect nipple and the wisteria-covered streets winding down toward the harbor are purple veins on the bosom of the hill. It was in Molyvos that my first marriage ended and my relationship with Aviva began.

From time to time, to cool the hot emotions triggered by writing, I'd take a stroll through the backyard. The bougainvilleas were springing up, their stems winding through the lattice and rising above the level of the fences. I picked up the hose I'd attached to an outdoor faucet and gave the vines a squirt or two to complement the rain that fell so sparingly that winter. The gardener who had planted the bougainvilleas told me that the vines needed watering until they were established.

In the yard's harsh sunlight the huge, untrimmed trees seemed overbearing. My trained architect's eye registered that there was no intermediate scale of plants to mediate between them and the plane of bare earth. The old avocado tree was dropping its inedible fruit on the dry grass. Many of the avocados had been chewed by squirrels or pecked by birds; the fruit made a squishy mess when it hit the ground, forming greenish yellow lumps of slippery mush that stuck to the soles of my shoes. The birds and squirrels were also nibbling the rangy orange tree, dropping fruit onto the deck, splattering juice and pulp over the redwood planks. The lemon tree's trunk had been attacked by a revolting whitish fungus.

In addition, the garden was overrun by a host of spiders that spun webs wide as sails billowing gently in the breeze. The spiders, their beige bodies striped with black like miniature matelots, scurried up and down the rigging in constant agitation, especially when I accidentally became entangled in their sticky filaments. After each foray outdoors I would hurry back to my workroom and the shady comfort of my words.

ℰꙅ

This negative feeling toward the yard persisted for months, until a casual event opened my mind to its creative possibilities.

The local hardware store I frequented while we were renovating the house had a large plant nursery set off to one side. Most of the time I paid the nursery no mind, but one unseasonably warm winter afternoon I was drawn to its green dimness. I rested a moment in the roofed section that housed indoor plants and those that needed shade and felt immediately soothed, as if a cool hand had covered my sweating brow.

A faint, sweet scent made my nostrils twitch. I couldn't identify it at first, but it sparked a wave of nostalgia. Like Marcel Proust's famous madeleine, the smell provoked a memory of things past...

I'm in Spain three decades earlier, wandering the rocky fields on the outskirts of the small coastal town of Altea where my first wife, Janine, our two young children, Paul and Karen, and I have been staying for the past few years. I'm resting in the shade of a carob tree beside a narrow channel of running water. These *acequias* were cut by the farmers to direct water to their fields, and they make bright streaks of moving silver in the sunlight.

Beyond my small patch of shade, the fields are parched by the late summer drought. The glare is so harsh it hurts the eyes. I can smell my own sweat under my light shirt, and something else; something sweet and slightly sickly.

Above me, a carob tree dangles its twisty, crusted pods. In this section of eastern Spain, between Valencia and Alicante, the carob fruit is used in the manufacture of chocolate, as a replacement for expensive imported cacao. My kids love the grainy, pastelike texture of this substitute "chocolate," but I favor the carob for its biblical associations.

As the Mediterranean's oldest native fruit tree, older than the olive, grape, orange, and lemon that were introduced later, the carob is believed by some to be the manna that fell from heaven to nourish the Israelites in the Sinai desert. It's also the bread that fed Saint John; the local name for carob is *pan de San Juan.* I idly break open a pod and a warm sticky smell fills my nose...

As my attention returned to the plant nursery, I searched for the smell that had triggered my reverie, but I couldn't trace it. "Perhaps it's the Arabian jasmine," the nurseryman suggested. I sniffed the vine he showed me, plunging my nose among the small white flowers. The jasmine's scent was sweet, but too refined, too perfumed. The smell I was after was much earthier and more crude, and somehow more nourishing.

I sniffed my way among the vegetation, hunting for that evocative aroma like a pig rooting out truffles. I stuck my hungry nose among gardenias, figs, and Hawaiian plumeria, and into the small bush called banana fig whose creamy yellow flowers give off a fruity scent. A Burmese honeysuckle with slender, curving, hornlike flowers had some of the carob's raw sweetness, but none of its dusty treacliness.

In the end I bought one of each of these plants and carried them home in my car. I hoped that, together, they might combine their smells to something that approximated the nostalgic St. John's bread; but in the closed car the various aromas made an olfactory chaos, as if a woman had spilled all her perfumes, creams, and lotions over her dressing table.

I set the plants in a corner of the garden, then forgot about them, except to add water from time to time. The novel continued to flow, words flowered on the page, and paper seemed a far more fertile soil than the baked ground in my yard. Each time I passed the plants on my infrequent visits outdoors, their jumbled fragrance seemed to mock the scent-memory in my mind.

I noticed, though, that the yellow horns of the Burmese honeysuckle had attracted a pair of hummingbirds. Zipping in and out in iridescent streaks of green and purple, the birds stabbed their needle beaks deep into the flowers' hearts. Their invisible wings made an intense buzzing sound, as if the tiny creatures were always furious. Every move they made seemed fierce and aggressive, especially when they chased one another around the garden like miniature fighter jets in a supersonic dogfight.

ॐ

One morning in early spring, when the words were slow to come, I drifted out into the garden and began to play at arranging the plants, which were still in their plastic pots. I found a spade and a bag of mulch the gardener had abandoned in the little shed at the bottom of the yard, and tried to dig a hole to plant the jasmine. But the long-neglected ground was so rigid and unyielding it bounced the spade's steel, and I soon gave up.

Instead, I took a pad and idly began to draw a

plan of the yard. I measured off the width and depth with a tape. The yard was an oblong, forty feet wide and sixty feet deep, with the southeast corner taken out for the guest house and its patio. I drew in the tall avocado tree, the banana palm, and the orange and lemon trees.

While I was sitting and sketching on the deck steps, it suddenly occurred to me that a garden could be imagined as a kind of "green" novel. The various zones suggested by the shape of the yard and the placement of the existing trees could be chapters organizing a green plot. Clusters of planting could be thought of as paragraphs, single plants as sentences or phrases that moved the garden story along.

I fancied that each plant would have its own expression—its own particular way of manifesting its stems, stalks, leaves, and flowers, its own rate of growth and potential size and presence. Collectively, plants, shrubs, and trees could be manipulated to compose a host of themes woven together into a vivid horticultural narrative.

Excited by the idea, I saw that my yard easily fell into visual chapters. One chapter opened directly off the main deck. Beyond it, at the back of the yard, separated by the avocado and an orange tree, was another, smaller chapter in this potential verdant tale. Yet another began beside the outdoor dining deck beside the kitchen. The two decks, back and side, offered further narrative sequences.

Each part of this green novel could have its own tone, its particular quality of light and shade through various times of the day. Facing east, the yard was also open to the sky on the north and south. The central chapter, on the north side, got the full sun on its left flank, except for the shadow of the avocado's umbrella. The back section, to the east, was sunny from dawn to midday. The third area, on the south, had light from the middle of the morning to sunset.

At this stage, the idea of a garden as a green novel was just that—a concept more than a spur to action. Characteristically, I read up on the history of horticulture before I could even think of actually getting my hands dirty.

In these readings I discovered that gardening had been conceived as a narrative art from horticulture's earliest origins. The ancient Chinese had subtly edited nature's wild story with a punctuation of delicate bridges, sinuous rills, and tiny islets. Over the following millennia, Egyptian, Japanese, Persian, Roman, Arab, Indian, Italian, French, Dutch, and

English gardeners had pursued the notion of garden as narrative.

Many of these horticultural plots are epic in scale and ambition, notably the Generalife gardens in Granada or Lenôtre's Versailles. Other green books are subtle and serene, like the Villa Lante near Viterbo, the Moghul Shalamar Bagh in Kashmir, or the Sento Imperial Palace grounds in Kyoto. Some, like Dutch domestic gardens, are tidy homilies bound by box borders and punctuated by clipped yews. Other gardens, like Kyoto's Ryoanji, are sleek haikus in rock and gravel spelling out "dream-of-heaven." Others point toward the Underworld, as in the Elysian Fields at Stowe in southern England. Or, like William Shenstone's the Leasowes, near Halesowen in the English Midlands, they mimic ruin-pocked, mock-Gothic melodramas.

There are gardens conceived as galleons calling you to fantasies of ocean adventure, like Lake Maggiore's Isola Bella, or the stone boat anchored off the shore in Florida's Vizcaya. Yet others are intimate plots for homebodies, tales to soothe the soul and calm the troubled mind. And then there are gardens as rough yarns or wild fictions to set the heart thumping, such as the sublimely "terrible" gardens of China described by Sir William Chambers, the eighteenth-century English traveler, with their "colossal figures of dragons, infernal fiends, and other horrid forms."

One of the most gifted of all green novelists was the eighteenth-century English landscapist Lancelot "Capability" Brown. Brown's Stourhead House in Wiltshire is a superb pastoral romance; a wide, rolling tale of an idealized serenity set with classical pavilions, arched bridges reflected in still pools, and rustic cottages hidden in bosky nooks. Stourhead is a series of living tableaux, an artful reimagination of a mythical Arcadia.

So, what story might my own green novel tell, I wondered. Would its compact space be crowded with a variety of texts, a narrative jumble running from lush passion to dry irony? Or would it be ordered by some overriding theme? Would it be romantic or sober, Dionysian or Apollonian, chaotic or serene . . . ?

That is, supposing I ever began to make the story happen with my hands, not just my head.

2

Countries of the Mind

A host of images floated around in my mind as I played with the plot of the story that might be composed upon the blank page of my yard. It was an idle daydream still, for I had as yet no intention of actively starting to garden. I was bound by a kind of inertia that prevented me from plunging wholeheartedly into horticulture. Besides, I was still engrossed in trying to make sense of Los Angeles and its fascinating physical and emotional landscapes.

In my travels around the area as a journalist seeking out interesting architecture, I had observed that any story one cares to imagine or compose is possible in southern California, given the will and the imagination. Los Angeles is altogether an act of imaginative, willful invention, a habitable fantasia written large in a semidesert landscape transformed by the importation of water from sources in the sierras and deltas hundreds of miles to the north, and from the Colorado River to the east. So many species of plant and tree in southern California have been introduced from outside, from places as distant and different as Malaysia, Australia, Hawaii and the Pacific Islands, the Mediterranean, South America, Europe, and Africa. Every foreign plant and tree seems utterly at home, while the native chaparral of scrub oak, toyon, sagebrush, wild lilac, California poppy, and manzanita has retreated to the barren hills.

Here can be seen every type of natural narrative, from the Amazonian to the Saharan. In the plant world, as in the human, Los Angeles is the territory of the self-invented dreamer, a country of the mind where anyone may create any naturalistic or surreal scenario imaginable.

D. H. Lawrence, visiting in the 1920s, succinctly characterized L.A.'s psyche as "sort of crazy-sensible," and for me the true grit of Los Angeles is its frank display of the social schizophrenia rampant in every modern city. Here madness and blandness, wackiness and smugness gallop along in tandem, and few Angelenos find such pairings odd.

"Sort of crazy-sensible" sums up L.A.'s visible urban style as well. On the main boulevards the bill-boards, constructed of steel, seem far more permanent than the gaudy plywood shacks housing shops, cafes, and fast-food joints huddled below. The unabashed, vigorous trash of the city's commercial strips jostles polite suburban avenues lined with skinny palms, bushy camphors, and, on the hillsides, solemn cypresses. In this wonderfully muddled context you may find a superb Craftsman bungalow from the early 1900s, a fine Art Deco or Streamline Moderne shopfront or store from the 1920s and 1930s, or a gracefully romantic Spanish Colonial Revival apartment block.

Just as your eye has come to accept the banalities of this jumbled cityscape, an act of sheer, delightful playfulness jumps out at you in the form of a hot dog stand shaped like a hot dog, a streamlined 1950s coffee shop lifted straight out of a futuristic cartoon, a portholed Coca-Cola factory mimicking the decks of an ocean liner, a hillside flying-saucer of a house hovering above a single concrete post, or an aerospace museum with a real jet fighter clinging to its front facade. One of my favorite L.A. places was a downtown porno cinema configured like an Aztec-Mayan temple, populated with lurid and ferocious effigies of Huitzilopochtli and Texcatlipoca glowering down through the erotic gloom upon a mesmerized audience.

But my most riveting crazy-sensible L.A. image

was the sight of a Rolls Royce quietly on fire one afternoon in the driveway of a mock-Tudor Beverly Hills mansion.

Here on an unpeopled, palm-lined avenue, the $250,000 automobile's glossy paintwork was blistering, its fat tires melting into black goo. Yet not a soul took notice, but for me. I stopped my car to watch the reflections of the yellow-orange flames flickering in the mansion's leaded windows, lighting up its eyes in the bright sunlight. I looked on in fascination as the shatterproof glass of the Rolls's windshield began to crack and crumble in that small holocaust of conspicuous consumption.

ॐ

However entranced I might have been by such superb crazinesses, when it came to buying a house, the choice was made for quite sensible reasons. Aviva and I chose Hollywood because house prices there were rather lower than in the more fashionable sections of L.A.'s Westside. But I'd be lying if I said I wasn't drawn by the lingering mythic glow the district still evokes, despite years of urban decay.

"Hollywood" is one of those stubbornly magic words no brute reality can quite seem to corrupt.

Our section of Hollywood, an historic area known as Spaulding Square, was subdivided in 1914. Its shady streets south of Sunset Boulevard, canopied by camphor, pepper, jacaranda, and magnolia trees, are lined with houses in a cheerful potpourri of styles, including a modified form of California Bungalow, a sprinkling of clapboarded Colonial Revivals and stuccoed Spanish, the odd Chicago Prairie School mannerism favored by the young Frank Lloyd Wright, plus one or two vaguely Italianate villas and English Revival cottages. Looking up from these cool avenues you can see the Hollywood Hills which, facing south, are bright with sun all day.

Spaulding Square is surrounded by landmarks of the old Hollywood. To the east, on La Brea Avenue, Charlie Chaplin founded his first studio in 1918, where he filmed *The Gold Rush* and *City Lights*. His son, Charlie Chaplin Jr., once occupied a house on Ogden, one street west of us, and committed suicide there in 1968. Lucille Ball lived a few doors down.

In the late 1930s, F. Scott Fitzgerald and Sheilah Graham would spend an intimate hour in the legendary neighborhood Schwab's drugstore, now demolished. Fitzgerald breathed his last in Graham's nearby Hayworth Avenue apartment on a December day in 1940, leaving behind an unfinished manuscript, later published as *The Last Tycoon*.

When we moved into the district, western Hollywood had been in decline since the 1950s and many middle-class families had moved away. The core of Hollywood Boulevard had long succumbed to sleaze and crime.

In the mid-1980s, the mythical resonance of the name had little to do with the mundane reality of the place. Parts of Hollywood, especially the eastern section, were tough as nails. Populated with an uneasy mix of Latinos, Armenians, Russians, Chinese, Filipinos, Thais, and Arabs, it was often riddled with gang gunfire. The area's polyglot babel was reflected in the enrollment at Hollywood High, the famous school where movie stars sent their children in the 1930s and '40s; in the late 1980s, Hollywood High counted around eighty different languages and dialects spoken by its students.

Hollywood Boulevard, in its famous central section between Vine Street and La Brea Avenue, a half-mile east of our neighborhood, is a surreal confusion where myth and reality collide yet somehow manage to cohabit. During the day, eager, camcorder-slung tourists from all over the world stroll the star-stippled Walk of Fame, jostling homeless kids, Mohawked freaks, wacked-out weirdos with rings through their lips and tattoos on their cheeks, and dazed mental patients pushed out on the street by brutal public policy. On the sidewalks, vendors sell maps to stars' homes that are about as up-to-date as Ptolemaic charts of the heavens.

After dark, the night people rule. Prostitutes, druggies, schizophrenics, and just plain desperate folk populate hangouts serving dishwater coffee and cheap chili dogs whose stink would fell a horse. Drawn by Hollywood's lost yet lingering glamor, old and young, male and female, gay and straight, black and white congregate on the corners, seeking the comfort of bright lights and the company of their peers. Now and then a blood-chilling scream slices through the buzz of chatter and the blast of rock rhythms, then falls away ignored.

Along with the rest of the district, Spaulding Square was dragged down by Hollywood's bad repu-tation. In the early 1980s, however, artists, screen-writers, and designers began to recolonize the leafy lanes west of Spaulding Avenue. They established a close-knit community in which neighbors watch out for one another and combine to protest to the police or the local city councilman if the tarts on Sunset get too brazen or too numerous.

1350 North Genesee Avenue was built in 1922, in the cottagey English Revival style popular in Los Angeles in the early decades of the century. It is a three-bed, two-bath bungalow with a steep, asphalt-tiled roof and white stuccoed walls. On one side is a carport, and at the back is a garage that's been converted into a small guest house. The one distinguishing feature is the large living room with a high, curved ceiling, a room that has the air of belonging to a larger, grander house.

As soon as we moved in, we renovated the kitchen and the bathroom, perking them up with colorful Mexican tiles. We extended the deck around the side of the house to link up with the kitchen, and added another section in front of the master bedroom so we could sit outside under the orange tree. It was under the orange tree that I dreamed away the hours imagining the green novel I might create sometime in the vague future...

৯০

One reason why my garden story was slow to take shape on the ground was the emotionally charged

24

memory of my father and his role as a gardener in Southern Rhodesia, now Zimbabwe, where I was born and raised.

My father was an avid horticulturist, yet he seemed to get little sensual pleasure from cultivating his flower beds. The look on his face was joyless as he labored in the African sun, stiffly dressed in a navy blue Matabeleland Tennis Club blazer and iron-creased gray flannels.

He spent most of his working life as a minor bureaucrat on the staff of the Rhodesia Railways. Beginning as an office boy at the age of thirteen, he'd painstakingly worked his way up to the position of chief clerk in the chief engineer's department. In truth, his whole life was an act of social and emotional mimesis. Like a chameleon, he, the son of immigrant Galician Jews, took on the protective coloring of the ruling British colonials, adopting their blazers and flannels, and their fierce dedication to the distant Crown in Westminster. Above all, he mimicked their narrow colonial notions of propriety.

My mother was something else. The eldest daughter of a large Ukranian Jewish family growing up poor in Bloemfontein, the capital of the South African province of the Orange Free State, she'd learned to fight on many fronts. She had battled daily with her autocratic father and fanatically religious brothers on one hand, and with the neighborhood Afrikaner anti-Semites on the other. Her tongue, sharpened to a razor's edge, could cut to the bone.

Rebecca Goldman was twenty-seven and thriving as the head of a typing pool on *The Outspan*, a popular national weekly magazine, when she fell for Charles Whiteson, a shy young man visiting Bloemfontein as a member of a Matabeleland tennis team. In an act of total perversity, that tough-minded young woman gave up her career and her independence to become the discontented wife of a lowly railway clerk in remote Bulawayo, the southern African equivalent of, say, Fargo, North Dakota.

"We Goldmans enjoy being perverse," my perverse Uncle Meyer told me once. "It gives us pleasure, and keeps us in a rage." Rage, he implied, was the only true response to the futilities of the human condition.

My mother's emotional ferocity only served to thicken my father's armor; he deflected her sharp barbs with a shield of nonresponse. Under attack, his face, with its big nose and hooded, kicked-puppy eyes, became shuttered with hurt restraint. He turned to nature for consolation, to our scrap of yard marooned in the reaches of the Rhodesian savanna. The garden was his refuge from both the household's tense domesticity and the surrounding African wilderness.

Yet his garden failed him. Somehow, despite his intense attention, his passionate pursuit of the perfect soil mix and avid searching for just the right species of rose, carnation, iris, petunia, delphinium, tulip, snapdragon, and chrysanthemum, the whole was always less than the sum of its parts. His garden seemed always too contrived, too prissy, too fearful of wildness to express the murky convolutions of his soul. Mostly it resembled a miniature front-yard Versailles, complete with neat brick allées and symmetrical, regimented flower beds lined up like guardsmen. Snapdragons snapped to attention like dragoons on parade; columns of Dutch irises stood stiff-necked in rows, while phalanxes of tight-lipped tulips marched toward the horizon alongside arrogant grandifloras and showy hybrid tea roses.

To me, my father's garden unwittingly laid bare his heartfelt *weltschmerz*, his sentimental pessimism and tragic sense of life's attrition. He kept a copy of Richard Jefferies' *The Story of My Heart* on his study desk, and one of the opening sentences was underlined: "For there is a dust which settles on the heart as well as that which falls on a ledge." Later in the text my father had marked the following passage: "It is eternity now. I am in the midst of it. It is about me in the sunshine; I am in it, as the butterfly floats in the light-laden air."

As the butterfly floats in the light-laden air. . . Hearing this phrase again in my head, the pathos of my father's yearning gave me pause. His fate haunted me; for a long time I feared it might be my own. He was a lover, but a lover without luck.

His lucklessness undermined even his small struggles against the natural insurrections threatening his fragile green world. No matter how hard he fought against the lizards that indolently sunned themselves on his brick paths, against the caterpillars that lusted for his leaves and the termites that tunneled under his soil, bursting through the manicured surface with their untidy mud mounds, he always seemed one battle behind.

His worst enemy was the host of voracious African grasshoppers that chewed up his roses. He struck back by plucking the insects from his blooms with a wooden clothes peg. With his nose fastidiously crinkled, the peg with its wriggling victim held at arm's length, he would drop the hapless creature in a bucket of water to drown.

His satisfaction with these small acts of killing was always intense. He saw his grasshopper drownings as "scrupulous," a carefully calculated response to a particular menace. Overall spraying with insecticides was anathema to him since it eliminated good bugs and bad without discrimination; such a strategy was thoroughly "unscrupulous"—his favored term of absolute condemnation.

However, he didn't object when the Ndebele servants retrieved the drowned grasshoppers, grilled them on a hot tin plate over a wood fire, and relished them as delicacies. In a gardener's terms, he explained, the insects were pests; in the natives' terms, they were a useful source of protein and fat in a limited diet of corn meal, and that made their actions as scrupulous as his. (The grilled grasshoppers tasted, I remember, like crunchy peanut butter mixed with bone marrow.)

When I was a boy watching my father garden, I always felt a current of suppressed sadness coming off his stiff body. He was a sentimental man whose sentiments had curdled in his breast, and the tears locked up in his heart were bitter. Even at the time, I wished he'd cry openly, to water the flowers he tended with such hopeless affection.

I only saw him cry once, and that was an odd occasion. He wept in public, and I was so embarrassed I could have killed him on the spot.

It happened at the circus, when I was nine years old, in 1940. The shabby Circo Gonzalez, advertised as "An International Travelling Show," somehow found its way from Andalusia to Bulawayo in the midst of a world war.

The once gaily painted performers' caravans and animal cages looked as if they had run a gauntlet of shot and shell. The circus tent, with its faded stripes and battered poles, was ripped in several places and seemed hardly larger than the Boy Scout tents we used for camping in the bush. A film of dust and decrepitude covered the hard wooden benches circling the sawdust ring.

My father clung to my hand as we found our seats in the crowded arena. His eager eyes drank in every detail of the scene, from the rusty iron bars caging a mangy lion to the overweight Gypsies in ragged costumes who crisscrossed the central circle of sand in an aimless pattern.

His palm was sweaty and anxious; I wriggled free of its clutch as soon as I decently could. "It stinks in here," I grumbled, wrinkling my nose at the stale smell of animal droppings, dust, and old sweat. My father ignored me, intent on his anticipation of promised marvels.

It was clear from the kickoff that the Circo

Gonzalez was a shambles. The aging strongman wrapped an iron bar around his neck and couldn't remove it until a dozen men from the audience jumped into the ring to help him. For a moment, as the group struggled with the stubborn bar, it seemed the old fellow might choke to death on his own foolishness.

The overweight lady acrobat had a dark mustache that twitched in panic as she wobbled on the trapeze wire strung a bare seven feet above the sand. Her skinny husband, arrayed in tattered motley, hovered underneath her, ready to catch his hefty beloved if she fell, though his chivalry might cost him his life.

The barrel-shaped lion tamer, got up as Tarzan, had the wary, spavined look of a failed wrestler. His lion skin costume was as patchy as his big cat's mane, and the beast seemed too bored to fear his cracking whip. Yawning hugely, the lion finally climbed onto a stool, tired as a drunk in a bar.

The clowns were so inept and frenzied they scared the watching kids with their antics. One clown, leaping over two rows of spectators to land with a resounding thump in the aisle, rose proudly with a bloody nose that might have been broken.

A strangled sob at my side interrupted my cringing fascination with this spectacle. Tears were pouring down my father's cheeks! Lord help me if he wasn't weeping for the strongman, the lady acrobat, the lion tamer, and the clowns, mourning their brave ineptitude and the circumstances that compelled them to display it. Intuitively, I understood that he saw something of himself in their humiliations.

But mainly I was horrified and deeply mortified. How could he be so slushy? How could this man, who never wept, betray us both in this unseemly fashion *in public?* How could he choose this time and place to let go?

I glanced quickly around to see if his shameful display was noticed by our neighbors, but everyone was too involved with the antics in the ring. I writhed with an embarrassment so acute I could cheerfully have fed my dad to the toothless old lion.

Slush-hound! I shouted soundlessly. *Howler!*

Perhaps he heard me. He turned his wet cheeks and smudgy eyes to me and murmured piteously, "My boy, my boy . . ." He hugged me hard, and I endured his embrace, feeling sulky and mean.

3

Opening Chapters

Five decades later, in the spring of 1988, I began to think differently of my deceased father. As I grow older I have more sympathy for his softheartedness, which has come to seem as much a matter of tenderness as "slush." There's a lot of him in me, I recognize, though braced by that "smidgeon of backbone" my mother once said might—and she emphasized *might*—save my life.

I wanted to reach out and touch my father's unhappy spirit in some way, and gardening seemed to offer a connection, a likely way to make a long-delayed peace with his memory. Perhaps, if I overcame my fears about following in the man's footsteps, I could make some kind of contact with him, touch that melancholy butterfly fluttering "in the light-laden air." So, overcoming my inertia, I started to come to grips with the challenge of my yard.

Certain features were given, I saw. The linked branches of a stunted orange tree and the lower limbs of the tall avocado formed a natural arch dividing the back area of the yard from the middle. The deck steps made an easy transition down to the ground, acting as a curtain raiser opening the inside to the outside.

Other sequences became obvious. A pathway of stepping stones from the deck steps would make a graceful curve toward the archway between the orange and avocado trees, echoing the line of the trellis separating the yard from the guest house patio. Along its length a series of individual enclaves seemed to suggest themselves.

Once the main pattern was established, other elements could be elaborated, such as the screen formed by the north fence. The bougainvilleas planted there were flourishing, suggesting a wall of thorns and flowers hidden from the garden's center. Another space was offered by the dark corner shaded by the guest house, yet another by the edge between the tool shed and the morning glory–covered back wall.

I put in a redwood archway between the orange and avocado trees and laid out a pathway linking it to the deck steps. I set the archway's ribs in concrete bases for permanence, and spaced out the round, pebbled-cement paving stones. Each paving stone had to be lugged from the back of my car and anchored in an individual cavity cut in the yard's stiff clay. There were forty-two stones in all, and putting them firmly in place was hot and arduous labor.

The long-neglected ground was so hard it resisted shovel, spade, and fork. Much of the time I had to soak it with the hose, then kneel and hack at it with a short-handled hoe or pick. I found much pleasure in striking the earth, revealing its rich underworld of worms as the ripe smell of turned-over soil twitched my nostrils and mud spots splattered my cheeks. After hours of such toil I was dirty but happy.

Digging in the yard was a relief from the tension of tapping at a keyboard. Words were airy ghosts but the soil had a brute concreteness, and all the stress of wrestling with verbal abstractions was soaked up by the honest sweat generated by hacking at the earth. Soon the counterpoint between toiling at my typewriter and laboring in the yard became a regular rhythm; there was a balance to it, a pleasing back-and-forth between mental and physical activity that drained my head and left my muscles pleasantly tired.

I found, too, that gardening is a delightfully childlike form of adult play, a chance for grown-ups to mess about in the mud without seeming silly. Digging in the dirt, I could imagine I was back in kindergarten or happily building sand castles on the beach. Unlike more fussy forms of adult play, like boating, say, or woodworking, which require elaborate equipment or implements, gardening can be accomplished mostly with that simple tool of childhood, the spade.

After erecting the central archway and laying out the pathway, I radically cut back the overgrown existing yard trees. Perched precariously on a tall ladder, I trimmed the avocado's trailing branches and shaped them into a neat umbrella to shade the central space from the hot afternoon sun while still allowing light to flood the area at dawn and dusk.

I chopped the ragged banana leaves back to the palm's stem to remove their clutter and stimulate fresh growth. I sawed dead branches from the orange and lemon trees, cutting them back to their bare bones. I cultivated their root systems with mulch and fertilizer, and hoped for a better crop than the shriveled fruit the trees had squeezed forth in earlier seasons. I sliced the grapevine back to its roots and tore out the clinging tendrils that threatened to strangle the big orange tree over the bedroom deck.

All this foliage had to be divided up into neat packages ready for the garbage collection. It was hard labor, sometimes even dangerous. On several occasions, struggling with a recalcitrant tree branch, I almost fell off the ladder. A ten-foot plunge to the ground could easily have broken an arm or leg, or even my neck. Once or twice a twig tried to poke my eye out, until I took to wearing protective goggles. Another time a hard, unripe avocado hit me on the head with such force I was momentarily stunned.

Despite these minor dangers, I enjoyed cutting a clearing in this tangle, making a blank page ready to receive my composition. Having asserted my presence, I could assume the authority of an author. And there was the even more primitive pleasure of doing violence to nature to test the true strength of its resolve. Once this honest and brutal intimacy has been established, a true sympathy may grow.

After a few weeks, my yard looked as bare as a blank page. The redwood archway, concrete paving stones, and dug-over earth had the air of a story about to be written—but what story?

Lacking a coherent plot, I knew the only way to go was just to plunge right in. I'd sometimes started a novel with no more than the single seed of an idea and had seen it grow into a book. All at once the germ of my idea yearned to be planted in the actual ground, and I was in a hurry to see the green narrative unfold.

I scoured the local nurseries—there were close to a dozen within a twenty-minute drive—and returned with carloads of plants. The interior of my small Nissan Sentra hatchback, layered with leaves and fallen blossoms, took on a permanent smell of mulch.

I bought plants indiscriminately, without fore-thought or foreknowledge. All I needed to know, all I wanted to know, was whether the vines, flowers, shrubs, and bushes required shade or sun, much watering or little, acid soil or alkaline. I happily traded the dead green dollars for the live green fo-liage, and felt I'd made a tremendous bargain. As soon as I got them home, I put the plants in the ground or into red clay pots.

It could be said that, as a budding horticultural-ist, I was protected by my ignorance. Since a novice gardener can be thoroughly daunted by dipping into gardening books that seem set upon making the process frighteningly complicated and fraught with failure, I deliberately avoided them. Many of these texts go on at length about such factors as climate zones, soil qualities, planting mixes, drainage prob-lems, weeds, and fertilizers. They warn you about pests of every kind, from maggots to thrips; about fungus and virus diseases, from mildew to fireblight.

Even so seemingly simple a matter as watering is

made out to be a major source of plant failure. "The variable factors involved are many and complex," one popular garden book warns. These factors include the thirst of each particular plant, its age, the season, air temperature, time of day, the nature of the soil, and the way you water. The whole operation could be threatened by "drought or drowning," and some of the more pedantic books insist that the only way to avoid these disasters is to engage in a deep study of the interaction between plant roots and soils.

My instinct was to learn by trial and error. Since most newly transplanted flora requires lots of watering, I had few failures. Some plants did die on me, but I learned from my errors, and in the process developed a hands-on feeling for the needs of each one. In this way I established a nurturing intimacy with everything I put in the ground or in a pot.

However, I did make some elementary mistakes. I grossly overwatered the gardenias until their leaves turned yellow and their blossoms blackened. I underwatered the hydrangeas; they shriveled up and died. I gave a pretty pink sun azalea so much Superbloom fertilizer it wilted from sheer excess of nutrition. But the sense of closeness I gained with every growing thing in my garden more than compensated for such errors.

Later, after I'd learned by doing, the information in garden volumes came to have real meaning. The knowledge my hands acquired gave life to the print. It was like making love to the first woman I ever knew, feeling out the sensual and erotic response of her body before reading any how-to sex manuals.

My priority was to develop a critical mass of greenery, to create a horticultural text that could carry its own conviction. The thing was to get it all down on the ground, make something happen out of nothing, as a writer does when confronting a blank page that may or may not come to be filled with phrases that have meaning.

While I kept adding new plants, most of the ones I'd put in the ground grew fast on a rich diet of fertilizer and copious watering. The yard's dark clay, rich with alluvial soil carried down by the Nichols Canyon flood plain to the north of us, responded rapidly to this nourishment.

The vanilla trumpet vine I placed beside the archway soon curved over the arch and sent out slender branches that entwined with the orange tree on one side and the avocado on the other. The vine, which put out small, scented violet-pink blossoms, thickened the screen of greenery dividing the center of the garden from the rear. This had the effect of making the yard seem larger, since you could no longer see where it ended up against the back fence.

Some plants provoked outbursts of memory, as if they were histories I'd known but had forgotten or not recalled for years. When I worked with them they seemed to speak to me, reminding me of my former selves in other landscapes.

For example, the three-foot-tall pencil tree, *Euphorbia tirucalli*, that I scavenged from a friend's garden evoked a vivid recollection of my childhood. In Rhodesia it grew as a common house hedge, and we kids used the sticky white milk that oozed from its broken green branchlets as a primitive glue. Mixed with mud, it stiffened the walls of the miniature forts we constructed, resisting the shot and shell of the little lead cannon balls we used in our war games. Now, feeling its milky latex go gluey on my fingertips, I was abruptly thrown back four decades, to the Matabeleland veld . . .

I'm sitting on a rock under a msasa tree. In the spiny branches overhead, among the pendulous, twisted pods, a male weaver bird is knotting together a nest out of twists of grass. Busy at his weaving, he ignores me as I rest.

On this spring October day the bush is so dry only

two colors rule the landscape: the bleached yellow of the scrub grass and the pale blue of the overarching sky. One lone acacia tree makes a silhouetted haiku in the middle distance. The far horizon is a dead straight line, and I'm reminded of Edward, Prince of Wales's remark that Matabeleland was, for him, "miles and miles of bugger all."

This landscape may seem flat and dead when, like the royal visitor, you hurry through it in a car. But if you sit down in it and wait, it comes vividly alive.

After a few minutes a scorpion emerges from under a stone. Its body is a squash of amber beads in the dust. It reaches out and touches its foreclaw to the toe of my tennis shoe, sleepily, for scorpions are night hunters who usually doze all day. I shift my shoe a fraction and the arachnid arches its stinger, a vicious probe aimed at my foot.

I freeze, my heart hammering; this scorpion's venom can easily pierce a canvas shoe and paralyze a grown man. I've seen an African stung once, and his agonized shrieks were hideous, as if he were being roasted by demons. But this creature backs off, and I can breathe easy.

Other insects come out to investigate me. Ants, spiders, beetles, crickets, centipedes, and millipedes scuttle about my shoes. My smell has drawn them; the odor of my sweat, earthy yet wet, that rises to my nostrils. They don't frighten me because, as an amateur entomologist, my sleeping porch at home is lined with their fellows preserved in smelly bottles of formaldehyde. My mother detests my *"verdamte goggas"* (damn bugs), as she calls them in the Afrikaans idiom.

Africa is owned by its insects. Its wild game may be spectacular, and nothing in the world beats the sight of a herd of antelopes or zebras pounding across the grassland, or a clutch of elephants cavorting at a waterhole; but the real rulers of this continent are the *goggas*, and they soon let you know it.

I pick up a millipede and watch it "swear"—twist and contort its black segments and red feet in a frantic attempt to scare away its predator. After a while, sensing I'm not repelled, the *shongalala* curls itself up in a tight volute and waits to die. When I put it back on the ground it immediately uncurls and wriggles away.

Another African memory triggered in my garden conjured up a summer when I hiked through the Transkei when I was an architecture student at the University of Cape Town. The Transkei, then a remote native reservation on South Africa's Indian Ocean coast, was inhabited by Xhosas who still wore their traditional home-dyed, blood red blankets to work in the fields, and painted their faces with reddish mud.

As I was striding along an empty road over rolling hills one hot afternoon my ears picked up a surprising sound: a folk song sung by women in the dulcet tones of well-bred English voices:

> Early one morning, just as the sun was rising,
> I heard a young maid sing in the valley below
> "Oh don't deceive me, oh never leave me,
> How could you use a poor maiden so?"

I hurried toward the lovely, limpid song, imagining for one wild moment that some posh British girls' school might be picnicking in this wilderness. The tune was so perfectly plaintive, the pitch so fine, the nuances so acute that I couldn't imagine any other explanation for that wonderful sound. But, cresting the rise, all I saw were a group of Xhosa women tilling the earth with primitive wooden hoes. The pure English melody, used as a work song to ease their labor, flowed from their mouths.

I knew that few of the Africans in this region

spoke English unless they'd been educated outside the reserve, in Durban or Port Elizabeth. None would have acquired such refined accents there. These women had clearly learned the tune and the words by ear with a superb gift of mimicry—but who from?

The answer soon appeared, in the form of a white man on horseback attired in a black cassock. Replying to my queries, the rider explained that he was a monk, a member of an Anglican Trappist order that operated a mission a few miles down the road. In a cultivated Oxbridge accent, the good father explained that the singing women belonged to the monastery's church choir. "They adore our hymns and country songs," he said, smiling. "Somehow the melodies suit this landscape as well as they fit the meadows of Berkshire."

He called out something in Xhosa, and the women laughed. Spontaneously, they switched at once to an Anglican hymn familiar to me from my Rhodesian morning school prayers:

> He who would valiant be
> 'Gainst all disaster,
> Let him in constancy
> Follow the Master.

I waved good-bye and walked on toward the next rise, followed by the hymn's brave tune.

❧

In the vicinity of the pencil tree I planted several hybrid abutilon shrubs (known popularly as Chinese lanterns) and trimmed them so they became either full-blown trees or canopies of vines supported on a network of plastic clotheslines strung between the fence and the house. I did the same with banksia roses, lavender starflower, Cape honeysuckle, and several varieties of jasmine, weaving their tendrils with the abutilon branches and the burgeoning bougainvillea to make a dense and shady cover over the pathway linking the deck steps with the center of the garden.

While these vines and shrubs were growing I populated many blank spaces with new trees and bushes. I found a rare yellow oleander bush in the college nursery in Pomona when I was invited to take part in a landscape architecture jury at the California state university. I bought a solanum tree from a nursery in Ojai, a hibiscus, a floss silk tree, and a princess flower bush from the arboretum in Arcadia, and azaleas, camellias, and gardenias at a sale in the

Huntington Botanical Gardens to provide a background for the more exotic varieties flourishing in my yard.

Whenever I went out on journalistic assignments I traveled with a spade in the back of the car. Some of my assignments took me far afield, into Ventura, Orange, Riverside, and San Bernardino counties, and if I saw a roadside bush of an unusual or visually compelling variety I quickly dug it up, furtive in my theft. I lifted specimens of Californian toyon, a bush with holly red berries. I spaded up laurel sumac shrubs, attracted to their reddish branchlets and aromatic foliage. I excavated a tree tobacco bush, drawn to the clusters of yellow flowers drooping from its rangy branches. The tree tobacco, originally from Argentina, has seeded itself so plentifully in the local landscape it seems like a native.

In the stretches of mountain and hillside that have not been developed, the region's native chaparral vegetation still survives the mass invasion of foreign plants. Dry, dusty, and tough, with hard green leaves and woody stems, the chaparral has for millennia vigorously come back to life after the brushfires that sweep the southern California slopes every summer.

The chaparral foliage is botanically "xerophytic," adapted to dryness with broad, hard leaves that retain water during the long southern California summers and frequent winter droughts. Fire renews this brush, and the Tongva and Chumash Indians who inhabited these plains and valleys before the Europeans arrived regularly purged the grasses and the chaparral with flames to stimulate a strong spring growth.

This maquis embodies the spirit of scrawny hardiness that lies under the watered green growth blanketing the built-up territory of Los Angeles County. The chaparral is the tough truth in this softened landscape—a truth that needs acknowledgement in any story about this place.

Chaparral gets its name from the *chaparro*, the local scrub oak. The scrub oak called to mind the Spanish *Quercus ilex* that the Castilian poet Antonio Machado made a symbol of endurance in the face of a harsh climate and harsher fate. However, while the Castilian ilex can reach up to seventy feet in height, the California scrub oak is a runtier version, really an evergreen shrub that seldom grows more than ten feet tall. In the Wild West, the *chaparro* gave its name to the leather chaps cowboys wear to protect their legs from thorns and prickles.

Spending so much time in my yard made me intimately aware of the Los Angeles sky's many moods.

At their worst, in high summer, the local heavens take on the aspect of an uncleaned, upturned toilet bowl. On such days the long, listless palms look like scruffy brushes scrubbing the smog-soiled sky. On the other hand, there's the subtle winter light when damp leaves after rain glisten in the mellow late afternoon sun and black wet tree trunks take on a coppery sheen. Then the air has the glow of old gold and the sky radiates a cobalt gleam.

On such days I could imagine I was back in Africa, standing beside my father in his garden, looking up at the wide blue vault of heaven washed by storms. I could almost believe, then, that I was close to him; even that I may have loved him.

4

Defending Boundaries

Late that summer, as the backyard flourished and became dense with a vigorous green, I began to be concerned with the neglected condition of the front of the house. The bare yard there exposed the facade to the street and left it naked to any stranger's view.

I began by planting some large trees on either side of the central pathway. To the left, looking from the sidewalk, I put in a scrawny young eucalyptus with silver dollar–sized ash gray leaves. The eucalyptus sprang up so quickly it curved over gracefully at the top, like a shy child hanging his head. Behind the eucalyptus, for contrast, I put in a deciduous liquidambar with maple-like leaves and a flowering plum that gave out shiny bronze foliage and pink blossoms in the spring. In the front I added a tender young red-barked camphor tree to match its huge mature brothers shading the street.

To the right of the pathway I planted a podocarpus with dense glossy green foliage next to a weeping cassia with clusters of bright yellow blooms. Beside the fern tree I placed a pomegranate tree that would bear its first heavy red grenades the following fall.

Nearer the ground, I lined both sides of the pathway with hibiscus, rockrose, magnolia, lantana, flowering pearl acacia, a rosemary-like Australian westringia, pampas grass, and veronica. I built an open redwood post-and-lintel gate halfway along the pathway and trained lilac-flowered hardenbergia and yellow cup-of-gold solandra up the sides and along the top.

ॐ

Working in the front garden brought me into contact with the life of the street and the people passing by.

The daily parade began early. Around six in the morning, when the day was fresh, a slim old woman with a red bandanna came by. My cheery wave was rewarded with a charmingly flirtatious smile and a steady, appraising look out of sage gray eyes. I discovered the old woman was Russian when, months after we'd established our little ritual, she suddenly said "Lovely morning" in a clotted accent. "Lovely!" I replied happily. After that brief exchange, she reverted to her mute and sexy smile, as if that were intimacy enough.

Not long after Red Bandanna passed, her well-fed compatriots appeared. Taking the morning air at a brisk pace in their trendy sweats, these Russians chatted at the tops of their voices, obviously delighted with their lot. By contrast, the bare-legged American joggers who outran them seemed grim with a determination to be fit even if it killed them.

Also grim in the early morning were the homeless men and women who haunted our neighborhood. There was the old woman pushing a supermarket trolley laden with old clothes; she seemed disturbingly like my old Jewish *bubba* with her swollen, varicose ankles and soft brown eyes that always seemed to be looking at another country of the heart. There was the excruciatingly polite young black man from New Orleans who slept under a spreading yucca bush near the local Bank of America, embarrassing his handout benefactors with effusive thanks. There was the young white man we called Full Metal Jacket for his uniform of camouflaged combat blouse and olive green steel helmet, who marched endlessly back and forth along the same stretch of Sunset Boulevard as if on guard duty. Sometimes he carried a thick stick, brandished like a carbine, that he used to shoot down imagined foes.

(After the April 1992 riots Full Metal Jacket came into his own. Assuming from his uniform that he was a member of one of the National Guard units summoned to restore order in Los Angeles, several strangers to the district patted the "soldier" on the back and thanked him fervently for his help.)

Every Thursday morning, just after dawn, a young man I dubbed the Scavenger came to scour the garbage cans put out on the sidewalk for the weekly collection. His face was youthful but grizzled and weatherbeaten from living rough, and his ripped leather bomber jacket seemed to have survived some bruising combat. While working in my garden I watched him take his pick of cans and bottles he could sell for pennies and load them into his battered shopping cart, which also housed his few possessions, including a constantly crackling radio and a large Tiffany lamp.

The Scavenger's personalized shopping cart was a symbol of the times. The carts were everywhere, serving as miniature moving vans for the homeless population of the streets or, as I once saw, used as an impromptu baby carriage. Covered with plastic

54

sheeting, the carts were often transformed into walls for temporary sidewalk shelters.

Despite their chromed-steel construction, the carts reminded me of ancient wooden barrows, recalling a preindustrial era before mechanization took command of our lives. Their owners, often dressed in a motley of rags, also seemed more like medieval mendicants than modern urban refugees.

An abandoned cart loaded with clothes and objects was a sad sight. I found one on our corner once, filled with a collection of split shoes, a worn sweater, and a cracked crocodile-skin purse that once, long ago, must have adorned the arm of a fashionable woman. Stuck in among these homely items was the dismembered arm of a shopwindow mannequin with the torn sleeve of a yellow blouse still attached.

Who might have abandoned that cart, and why? And why were these largely useless things collected in the first place? These questions went unanswered, and the cart's absent owner remained a haunting ghost.

Then there were the dogwalkers. Old Fred across the way emerged early on, tugged by his pair of eager, barking collies. Fred waved at me, panting with the

55

effort of restraining his frisky dogs. Sometimes, catching his breath, he would applaud my gardening efforts with a cheery "Good job!" Later, Pamela, the songwriter who lived up the street, walked by, following her two fluffy white Maltese toy dogs named Cuddles and Chance, who eagerly scampered up to sniff my toes.

The most touching dogwalker of all was Yvonne, a pretty, mentally retarded adolescent girl who, like Red Bandanna, was gifted with a glorious smile. Accompanied by her docile German shepherd, Yvonne lingered beaming and silent to watch me as I worked in the garden. She offered no words; I respected her reticence and always looked forward to her passing.

Other passersby were rich with chat. A plump, rosy-cheeked Frenchwoman, identifying herself as *une couturière stylistique*, rolled out long monologues on the art of horticulture that I only half-listened to as I toiled. Her Parisian lilt was like birdsong in my ear. Others, astonished that a homeowner would be doing his own gardening, especially the backbreaking work of digging and planting, stopped to question my intentions.

In our district, as in most of Los Angeles's largely white Westside, gardening was done by hired Latinos. Armed with noisy, polluting leaf blowers and sputtering, rusty lawn mowers, the men from Mexico, Guatemala, El Salvador, and Nicaragua tended the gardens their owners were too busy or simply too lazy to cultivate on their own. The Latinos' role, like that of the Africans in my native land, was to do the hard and dirty work whites found tiring or boring.

The result, to my eye, was a landscape of gardens well kept but unstroked by hands-on affection, like pampered kids whose parents were too busy to cuddle them. It's only by digging and sweating and watering each plant that any man or woman can make a garden truly their own child; only then can they legitimately call themselves the father or mother of their cultivated ground.

My front garden stuck out in the street and invited much comment from passersby because it was clearly cared for in a highly personal way. In place of the boring rose beds, bland lawns, or emblematic yuccas that covered many frontages, I had a wild assortment of vegetation. In fact, I detested most formal roses for their floral smugness, along with tulips, gladioli, and irises. To my prejudiced eye these flowers seemed irredeemably self-satisfied, unforgivably bourgeois. Most of all, I disliked the flashy agapanthus that decorated so many suburban front yards.

I also hated the neighborhood cats, who frightened away the birds and squirrels and yowled like banshees at mating time. The cats kept coming back, no matter how often and vigorously I chased them off.

I particularly loathed one fat black tom who acted as if he owned my garden. He found lordly perches on my trellises, or lay in wait under the bushes to leap out and kill some unwary sparrow or robin. I hunted him down with the hose, surprising him with a jet of water that sent him hissing, wet in flight.

No matter how often I chased him away, the tom kept coming back. He seemed determined to ignore my claim to sole command of the territory, and we developed a fierce feud. I took to stalking him in his hiding places with the hose held ready, like a rifle cocked to fire. Whenever I thought I'd finally driven him out, I'd see him perched in some new place, glaring down at me with yellow-eyed malice. In the end we came to a wary détente: I ruled at ground level, he ruled at trellis level, eight feet up.

Where I loathed the cats, Aviva took against the local dogs. She resented their incessant barking night and day.

Within a few months after we settled in, Aviva had made enemies of all the nearby dog owners. She persecuted them with phone calls and irate notes slid through their letterboxes. She threw Milkbone dog biscuits over fences to shut up the noisy hounds and scattered a foul-smelling canine repellent powder far and wide.

When the neighbors began to fight back against this reign of terror with angry phone calls of their own, Aviva became more devious. Disguising her Aussie accent with what she fondly imagined was a southern drawl, she took to phoning the dog owners anonymously, warning them that their "damn dawgs are drivin' me ker-razy." She boasted that she was getting away with this deception until she received an angry message on her answering machine from one neighbor. "I know who you are, Aviva Whiteson," the caller said. "Don't be so gutless!"

Aviva's antidog campaign left one touching memento. In a patch of cement I spread to repair a hole in our driveway is a canine pawprint beside the impression of the sole of one of Aviva's Birkenstock sandals. It records the moment that Aviva rushed out to harass a hound, and both of them left their marks for posterity.

❧

Working in the front yard also brought me into contact with a current of ugliness underlying the more amiable aspects of the neighborhood. It bubbled up strongly in an intensely divisive battle over the conversion of a local house into a hospice for AIDS patients. The antagonisms generated by this dispute polarized the district and roiled murky waters of bigotry and fear.

Conflict arose when a local homeowner surreptitiously leased his house on Ogden Drive, the next street over, to a nonprofit AIDS hospice organization. As soon as word of this got out, a vocal group of neighbors rallied to fight the hospice, and a countergroup was organized in support.

Some members of the antihospice Neighborhood Action Group, as they called themselves, feared that the conversion of a family home into a business of some kind would lower property values. Others could barely conceal their hatred of homosexuals. Several NAG members—dubbed "Nazi Aryan Group" and "Neighbors Against Gays" by their opponents—successfully petitioned the city's Board of Zoning Appeals to forbid the hospice, named Hughes House, in an area designated as R1 residential under the Hollywood Community Plan.

NAG members cooked up rumors that AIDS could

be spread by mosquitoes and that the local dogs could carry AIDS from house to house. They circulated a pamphlet, excerpted from Hansard, the transcript of debates in the British House of Commons, which claimed that AIDS-related tuberculosis could be disseminated by coughing and sneezing. (Hansard, like the U.S. Congressional Record, prints verbatim everything said in Parliament, no matter how vicious or silly.) "The war against AIDS is a war of survival," the pamphlet declared. Homosexuals, "seeing death and destruction facing themselves and their friends are dedicated to destroying the rest of society with them."

One irate neighbor, stopping to chat as I gardened, declared outright that "AIDS is God's punishment for sodomy." Quoting I Corinthians, she intoned, "Be not deceived: neither fornicators, nor idolaters, nor adulterers, nor effeminate, nor abusers of themselves with mankind...shall inherit the kingdom of God." Another passerby said, more crudely, "The wages of buggery is death."

Meanwhile, the prohospice Friends of Hughes House organized local and citywide support. The group marched on city hall to protest the zoning board's repeal of the hospice's permission to operate. As a result, the board later reinstated the hospice's permit.

While this was going on, the neighborhood was riven by meanness. One mysterious and misguided prohospice advocate, rumored to be terminally ill himself, slunk about the local streets late at night uprooting shrubs and smashing pottery planters. An agave cactus in my front yard was ripped from the ground and several terracotta planters on my front porch were shattered by this angry phantom. When Aviva went knocking on doors to collect signatures on a prohospice petition, she was bodily flung down the front steps by a furious neighbor.

One very respectable old lady, a longtime resident who lived across the way from the hospice, was dubbed a "lush" and a "slut" when she was seen carrying charitable offerings of milk and bread to the seven terminally ill men in Hughes House. Hospice opponents set up a steady surveillance, photographing the comings and goings of the dying and the dead as evidence for use in the zoning appeal. "It's like living in the shadow of death," complained one neighbor, whose house stood directly behind 1308 North Ogden. "There's this sadness in the neighborhood."

My wife and I attended a crowded meeting in a local church in which pro- and antihospice protagonists furiously shouted one another down. Accusations were traded about infected material tossed carelessly into the trash, about antigay slanders, about the deliberate rousing of hostility in the community by both factions. "This place just doesn't belong in a family neighborhood!" one angry resident declared.

The matter was resolved when the Board of Zoning Appeals voted to allow Hughes House to operate. In a Solomonic utterance, the chairman of the zoning board said; "I am going to ask the neighbors to sacrifice and give compassion to their fellow man."

♧

I think the real core feeling involved in the hospice dispute was never really brought out into the open: the urge to defend communal boundaries in a city becoming increasingly fragmented, tense, and hostile. These tensions, which literally burst into flame in the riots of April 1992, were already pressing upon our local borders; the entry of the AIDS hospice seemed to many a fatal breach of the perimeters that protected Spaulding Square from the surrounding dangers.

In this vast, inchoate, and often menacing metropolitan sprawl, many Angelenos are anxious to define their communities, to protect a particular sense of identity in the urban anonymity. Standing on a patch of one's own secure ground often seems the only safe way to negotiate with the rest of the megalopolis.

Since modern cities have burst their bounds and have become shapeless regional metropolises covering hundreds of square miles, no single citizen can hope to comprehend their enormity. Complex and confusing, these urban regions offer little sense of coherence when contemplated as a whole. The only way to cope with such vast social and geographic entities is to be rooted in your own defined, defended ground.

Defending one's boundaries, a necessity in a modern metropolis, is also an ancient impulse. In Hebrew, for instance, the root word for "garden," *gimmel nun nun* (rendered GNN in the Latin alphabet), also serves the verbs "to protect," "to surround," and "to defend." *Gan Eden*, the Garden of Delight, carries the implicit sense of a space walled against outside threat.

The high, overgrown walls of my garden secure me from two kinds of threat: from the immediate threat of burglary and break-in in this crime-ridden city, and from the more subtle menace of an invasion of privacy by that tense, dark world known as "the street." In making my private Eden I have drawn a line around my domain to mark the boundary between assured safety and likely danger.

This line circles the heart of most urbanites, especially Americans. In U.S. cities, the world "out there" seems fundamentally hostile, charged with potential chaos, totally unworthy of trust. Guarding the perimeters of one's neighborhood, garden, and house is vital for survival against the menace of the public realm, which so often reeks of poverty and dark failure. The private realm, the world "in here," is a separate space most urban Americans believe can only be surrendered at great personal risk.

The same holds true for Europe, despite its more popular and trusted civic realm. In many European cities private gardens and houses are hidden behind anonymous street facades punctuated by thick doors or heavy iron gates that can quickly be slammed shut against attack. Those homes that have no walls are usually equipped with iron bars or wooden or steel shutters that seal their windows tight.

In its essence, then, my small enclosed garden belongs to that timeless category of human settlement shaped by the threat of violence from one's fellows. It is a category as old as civilization. In the

65

era of prehistory men erected the Sardinian *nuraghi*, tall cones put together out of piled stones, markers of protection in a harsh landscape. Later came the Scottish rock citadels called *brochs*, and the populated volcanic cones of Goreme in eastern Anatolia. In the United States, between A.D. 1100 and 1300, the Anasazi peoples of the Southwest created the protected settlement known as Pueblo Bonito in New Mexico's Chaco Canyon and the dramatic cliff villages of Mesa Verde in present-day Colorado.

Whole towns and cities have been shaped by the threat of attack, from biblical Ur and Jericho to Homeric Troy, Byzantine Constantinople, and Ottoman Jerusalem, on to Muslim Baghdad and Marrakesh and Christian Avila, Toledo, Dubrovnik, and Carcassonne, plus such Tuscan towns such as San Gimignano and Siena. The iconic form of all these towns was configured by a sense of threat at every level of human experience. It is their creative response to threat that has given such places their superb architectural distinction.

Cities and citadels creatively shaped by threat derive much of their emotive power from the sharp contrast between the open safety of their interior streets and squares and the enclosed, defensive stoutness of their walls. Granada's Alhambra, for example, draws its visual drama from the contrast between the secure delicacy of its interior pavilions and the protective crudeness of its red stone battlements. Having crossed the open valley, under the looming white peaks of the Sierra Nevada, a visitor climbs a steep slope up to the foot of the citadel's cliff-like walls. He passes through an armored gate and is embraced by an oasis of civilization and safety.

Anyone who has walked the Alhambra's battlements and passed a quiet moment in its chambers and courtyards will appreciate this connection between massive protection against external threat and the tranquillity of spirit such security allows. "Deserted and roofless are the houses of our enemies, invaded by the fall rains, traversed by tempestuous winds," runs an anonymous ninth-century Andalusian verse. "Let them within the Red Citadel hold their mischievous councils, surrounded on every side by perdition and woe."

Sultan Boabdil, the Alhambra's last Moorish ruler, wept as he turned for a last look at the magnificent walled fortress he had just surrendered to the Christian forces of Isabella and Ferdinand. His implacable mother (who must have been rather like my own) told him, "You do well to weep like a woman for what you could not defend like a man."

Boccaccio's fourteenth-century Florentine nobles populating the *Decameron* sought refuge from the bubonic plague in a walled country garden. While the "death-dealing pestilence" raged in the city, "The merry company . . . went straying with slow steps, young men and fair ladies together, about a garden, devising blithely and diverting themselves with weaving goodly garlands of various leaves and carolling amorously." The young men and women passed their days telling stories to keep their minds off the horrors polluting the outside world.

An anonymous early-sixteenth-century Sufi poet expressed this feeling perfectly in his "Ode to a Garden Carpet":

> Beset by stalking Death in guises manifold;
> The dreaded jinns, the beasts ferocious,
> The flaming heat and the exploding storms,
> From all this peril here at last set free,
> In the garden all find security.

While making my garden I began to grasp a vital paradox: Only the safety and identity of an intensely personal private place within a clear community can encourage each citizen to reach out for a genuine connection with the city at large.

If this paradox had been openly discussed in our community during the AIDS hospice dispute, the warring neighbors might have been able to reach an honest compromise. The Neighborhood Action Group, which had successfully defended community boundaries against intrusion by prostitution, might have come to accept that the small seven-patient hospice would not destroy the district's identity or threaten its safety. The Friends of Hughes House, on the other hand, could have agreed upon reasonable standards of operation designed to upset the neighbors as little as possible.

In fact, this was the actual result of the hospice controversy. Hughes House, occupying a discreet small clapboard bungalow, has functioned with little fuss. However, if the boundary-defense issue had been directly addressed, the fires of bigotry and slander might well have been contained. Maybe I should have stood up and said this at the time. But I was still too new to the neighborhood, and I was only just beginning to grasp the issue of boundary defense in the Los Angeles of the late 1980s.

It's an issue that touches every Angeleno, regardless of social condition. For example, an attempt by the authorities to locate a new state prison in the midst of a working-class Latino district in East

L.A. provoked a vehement grassroots opposition that galvanized the whole Eastside and, after a six-year battle, ended in the project's cancellation.

Anyway, the specter of AIDS has taken up permanent residence in my garden; I have mementoes of three friends killed by the disease. I transplanted a pomegranate tree inherited from Marc, who died in 1993. I received a painted black and white plywood yard cow from Douglas, who died a few months earlier the same year, and I have a philodendron from Michael, who died in 1989. Memories of these three friends have become integral to the garden's texture.

5

Zones, Leaves, and Water

By the spring of 1989, twenty months or so after we'd moved into the Genesee house, both my green novel and my white novel were moving along in tandem. I shuttled between my Hollywood garden and an imagined Molyvos with the ease of a seasoned traveler in a space-time continuum, carried along by the momentum generated by both narratives. As I busily wrote and gardened, gardened and wrote, the emotional landscapes of Los Angeles and Lesbos began to fuse in my mind. The presence of Emma, the heroine of *Dreaming of You*, seeped from my pages into the garden; I fancied I could see her wandering naked as Eve through the greenery, her skin crossed with slats of sunlight coming through the leaves, the warmth of her body blending with the scents of jasmine, orange blossom, sweet olive, and honeysuckle in the spring heat.

Emma was based on Aviva, whom I met in Molyvos in the summer after my long marriage to Janine came to an end. The experience of falling madly in love for the first time in my life had shaken me to my roots.

I was introduced to Aviva on Molyvos beach by a mutual friend, who smoothed the way by telling her that I was an amateur palmist. The amiable chicanery of palmistry was a hobby of mine; reading hands was a way to get to know someone without appearing too nosy.

I saw at a glance that Aviva's small palm was limber and expressive. But I was more fascinated by her body. Small but sturdy, it had the rare quality of seeming absolutely at ease. There is often an edge of awkwardness in the way even women with superb figures carry themselves, and I'd thought such unease was inherent in the female condition. In Aviva, that awkwardness was absent. The spirit and the flesh were in tune, and to me that was so profoundly erotic I thought my heart would leap out of my mouth. The crazy thought flashed in my head that I had seen her figure in a dream, that Aviva had the form of some archetypal Eve swimming in my unconscious mind.

"Well?" Aviva demanded, rousing me from my reverie. "What do you see in my hand?"

Something in her eyes made me say, "You're on

72

the edge of an emotional abyss. You'll either leap over it, or fall into a bottomless pit." She jerked back her hand and a flash of anger darkened her green eyes. I'd penetrated her privacy and she didn't much like it.

We met casually in the village or on the beach several times in the following weeks. Aviva seemed wary in my presence, but every so often I noticed her looking at me with an odd expression. "Is this man a phony or the real thing?" her look asked. I had no ready answer, except that I felt my world was turning on a dime and that I had to make love to her or die.

When I told her this, she laughed. My candor disarmed her; she recognized there was a grain of truth in my declaration, as well as romantic hyperbole. "I can't think of anything else but your body," I said.

"No woman can resist a ploy like that," she answered. That night we became lovers.

❧

Aviva liked to mock my obsession with gardening. Every so often she'd wander through the yard, chiding me for all the time I put into its cultivation. Her mockery was fond, though. "If you have to have another woman, I'd rather she was leaves and bushes than flesh and blood," she'd say.

Her comment brought home the fact that I'd created an essentially feminine form out of all that bosomy foliage, a female configuration charged with all the passionate fondness and absolute affection I felt for Aviva and was trying to render in regard to my character Emma. The trees, vines, shrubs, bushes, and plants I'd crowded into my garden had created a magical presence all their own, a kind of green dreaming that assumed the glow and power of a woman's body.

The hard, cold ground I'd broken open with my spade was a metaphor for the carapace of defensive irony and disappointment I'd had to crack in order to love Aviva without holding anything back. The fertility of the freshly turned soil opened to the sun symbolized the rush of feelings released by the warmth of our passionate affections. The garden that flourished in the nurtured ground mirrored the greening of my lover's heart.

～✿

My garden's green heart was home to a variety of feelings, each with its own narrative character. Some sensations were intense and hot, others were cool and easy; some were intimate, others had an edge of threat. Altogether, they manifested the changes of mood and pace that charge any deep passion.

On a literal level, much of this variety was dictated by each zone's differing exposure to the sun. Other qualities were accidental, or perhaps intuitive, depending on the placement of certain highly individual plants.

The sun was the main elemental force shaping the garden. Since my yard was urban and in the Hollywood flatlands, it was protected from the worst violence of the hot, dry Santa Ana winds that blew down from the hills. Rain, often sporadic in southern California, was mostly replaced by watering. The rich black clay, responding to a generous fertilization, nourished any plant regardless of its location.

The sun, then, determined that some areas were bright, others dim, yet others temperate and soft with light. At the height of summer the sun traveled through a high arc of around 270 degrees, lighting up the garden at the east end of the north fence at dawn, and at the west end at dusk. At the winter solstice the sun's arc was flatter and tighter, rising over the east back fence and setting in the west behind the shadow of the house.

With this solar movement, the garden's entry beyond the deck steps took on a bright, almost racy tone. Sunshine poured into the clearing over a fringe of wild morning glory. The fast-growing vine, spilling blue-purple flowers over the top of the trellis, was tangled up in its greed to cover every surface within its grasp.

The morning glory set the tone there, but its presence was accidental. Its vines, rooted in the neighbor's yard, had simply claimed my trellis. At the same time it invaded a lonely cypress along the fence, bending the hapless tree double with the weight of its flowers and tendrils. Faced with such forcefulness, I humbly accepted nature's intervention, and tried to play with it and against it.

The large crown-of-thorns bush I placed at the edge of the clearing was my main counter to the morning glory's spread. Spiky and crisp where the morning glory was soft-edged and scruffy, the crown-of-thorns squeezed out neat scarlet bracts that resembled droplets of blood. The dynamic energy generated between these antagonists provided a tension that made entrance into the garden a sensual event.

The lavender starflower over the deck steps became entwined with the night-blooming jessamine and the coral honeysuckle, tightening the sense of entry. Its small, vivid pink blooms, peeping through the foliage, mingled with the white jessamine berries and the honeysuckle's clustered, yellow-throated flowers.

Later, I added a playful element at the side of this point of entry. A Christmas gift of a little red wooden engine and carriages was emptied of its candies and refilled with petunias, violets, and a clay goat; I nailed this jolly little train to the timber balustrade beside the deck steps, and next to it I added a green-painted wooden frog tapping a red drum.

The second zone unfolded along the length of the tunnel linking the deck steps to the central clearing. Roofed over with a tangle of yellow jasmine, abutilon, and bougainvillea vines, its tone was mottled. The next main area was the central clearing, sunny on one side, shady on the other. Its early growth of princess flowers, hibiscus, pencil trees, trumpet vines, and tree ferns suggested a complexity of themes, many of which had as yet barely surfaced in my mind or under my hand.

In the rear zone beside the back fence, bougainvilleas of varied colors covered a network of redwood joists, creating a natural tent. The area was deeply shaded, with long views back into the body of the garden through slits in the greenery.

Another enclave was created by one of those slits, twisting along the honeysuckle on the northern fence to a distant glimpse of light. In the darkest space of all, shielded from the sun by the wall of the guest house and a canopy of bougainvillea, lush, large-leaved ferns, dracaenas, bog plants, elephant's ear, Australian ginger (*Alpinia caeonlea*), and New Zealand puka shrubs (*Meryta sinclairi*) luxuriated in a tropical green wetness, conjuring up the sensation of a clammy rain forest charged with passionate life and provocative possibilities.

On the far back fence the blackberry bushes I bought in alpine Idyllwild put out small white flowers with papery leaves. The berries that followed were sweet as honey and tart at the same time, a delicious conflict on the tongue.

Blackberry bushes can get away from you and run wild if you let them, many garden writers warn. Let them get away, I say. In my garden untrimmed blackberry runners appeared in some startling places—dangling from an overhead trellis or self-planted among a patch of begonias. Like some long-legged spiders, they seem to glory in their freedom to investigate and colonize every corner.

All in all, I found I was more fascinated by leaves than flowers. Blossoms are pretty and touching, but, to my eye, leaves have a much wider range of expression. It is leaves that give most bushes, plants, shrubs, and trees their body and true presence. Leaves are the laboratories that convert water and sunlight into the sugars and carbohydrates that drive a plant's growth. Through the action of photosynthesis, the leaf's chlorophyll takes in carbon dioxide from the air and returns clean oxygen, and pushes the green force outward and upward.

Maybe my liking for leaves came from memories of many tramps through dewy English woods of oak, beech, and ash. In London, living near Hampstead Heath, I'd often escaped the city's buzz in that park's urban forest, where leafy foliage filters the misty English light, generating a dappled mystery.

Leaves come in a startling range of shapes and sizes, from those big enough to wrap a body in to others no thicker than a thread. They can be broad fronds or tiny stars, large green snowflakes or sharp needles; they can be tender or tough, vulgar or refined, yielding or resistant. They can stroke your cheek as you brush by, or scratch your eye. They can be bronzed or dead white or every shade of green.

They can be hairless or hairy, sharp in silhouette or fuzzy, glossy or pulpy, skinny or plump.

I soon discovered that the unfolding of new leaves is one of the most moving events a gardener can witness. Those marvelous revelations occur almost all year long, from February to November, and each one is as extraordinary as it is commonplace. A leaf's unfolding can be as simple as a fig's foliage opening up at a branch tip, or as startling as the new leaf splitting the stem of a tropical elephant's ear to emerge, like Eve, born from Adam's rib.

One of the most expressive unfoldings of all is that of the *Ficus religiosa*, the sacred fig known as the bo or bodhi tree. Twenty-five hundred years ago, according to Buddhist tradition, the Buddha found enlightenment (*bodhi*) under such trembling leaves.

A new bodhi leaf emerges from the growing end of a branch stem in the form of a pointed, pale green sheath. The new leaf, wrapped in a tight twist, pushes its way through the sheath and begins to uncurl. The tender thing is translucent as onionskin, fragile to the touch, silky against the fingertips. In a few days, stroked by the sun, the enlarged leaf lies flat and develops the texture of veined, olive green hide. The bodhi leaf ends in a slender tail, giving it the aspect of a fat green tadpole swimming in the air.

Wandering in the garden one late fall day, with my eye and inner ear adjusted to its harmonies of sight and sound, I gradually became aware of a certain absence. A crucial note was missing in my metaphor of the garden as a lover's heart—but what?

Slowly it came to me: There was no sound of water.

My garden needed fountains. It required that essential Mediterranean tinkle and splash cooling the air, soothing the heated mind, stroking the agitated spirit. On the rim of the fountain in the Court of the Lions in the Alhambra, an Arabic script compares the flow of water pushing up from the depths to "a lover whose eyes are brimming with tears."

Impelled by a kind of urgency, I quickly created several fountains in my garden. I bought four of the halved oaken whiskey barrels plant nurseries sell, plus a variety of small submersible electric pumps that recirculate fountain water. I acquired a concrete fish, a dolphin, and a cherub from yards that sold garden statuary, and arranged them so they spilled or spurted water at regular intervals through the garden. To the toy train on the deck balustrade I added a yellow milk jug shaped like a baby chick, which I converted into a spout sending an arc of water into a basin filled with bog plants.

I found I could "tune" a fountain's sound by adjusting the flow of water and the distance of the throw. The fish, spurting high in the air at full force, created a rapid drumming as its stream hit the surface of the water in its whiskey barrel. If I moved the barrel in closer, or cut the rate of flow in the pipe connecting the fish with its pump, the drumming softened its staccato percussion.

The cherub's spouting could be tuned in a range between a saxophone's gurgle and a triangle's tinkle, while the dolphin's flow was reedy as an oboe. I elaborated the dolphin fountain with the addition of a miniature water wall fashioned from a slab of black marble a neighbor gave me. I topped the marble with a perforated copper pipe that released a glistening sheet of water hissing down the slab's surface with a sound like a penny whistle. In this symphonic medley the spurting chick on the balustrade generated a high-pitched fluting, a plain copper pipe oompahed like a tuba, and a big white Bacchus face shot forth a stream trumpeting into the big round belly of an earthenware amphora.

By the time I was done, my garden was fugal. Wherever I stood I could hear a different counterpoint of water sounds. When I moved, this music altered its balance, beat, and texture, and no two places offered the same assonance or dissonance.

Choral comments upon the fountain themes came from the yawpings of scrub jays, the trillings of mockingbirds, the whirrings of hummingbirds' wings, the cooing of doves, the buzzing of bumblebees, the chirruping of squirrels, the squawkings of wild parakeets, the occasional squeals of hunting hawks, and the cicadas' summer night chirpings. Taken together, these bright sounds muted the rumble of traffic, the screech of sirens, the shouts of children, the barking of dogs, the outbursts of rock music, the clatter of a neighbor's pool pump, and the racket of gas-driven leaf blowers and mowers in the surrounding streets.

Something about the emotional nature of sounds became clear to me in this counterpoint. Seated in my garden, I could hear the drumming approach of a police helicopter or the roar and rattle of a passing garbage truck without becoming alarmed by the seeming prospect of invasion. The violence of the noise was gentled by the greenery and by the feeling that it would never invade my private place. On the other hand, some small, unidentified scrabbling within the boundaries of my garden walls could send a chill down my spine with its threat of close-up menace.

The fountains in my garden were a vital addition, for water is the emblem of Los Angeles's powerful will to grow. Without water, L.A. would have remained a collection of small towns scattered over the Los Angeles Basin and the San Fernando Valley, its growth stunted by drought.

In fact, the beginning of my garden coincided with the start of a six-year California drought that was eased by the spring storms of 1992 and finally broken by the torrential rains of early 1993. At the drought's height, reservoirs ran dry, garden water was rationed, and many lawns turned brown. Since I avoided wastage by hand-watering every plant, I stayed well within my ration. With their recycling pumps, my fountains wasted little water, apart from some evaporation and splashing.

To minimize the impact of such droughts, brutal L.A. water barons around the turn of the century had seized the resources of the Owens Valley river system hundreds of miles north of the young and expanding city. The ruthless water imperialism of Mayor Fred Eaton and city engineer William Mulholland forged the 232-mile aqueduct that sucked the Owens Valley lakes and rivers dry and pumped lifeblood into Los Angeles, powering its spread over hundreds of square miles of Southland wilderness and farming communities. Later, L.A. extended its water-grabbing tentacles to siphon moisture from the Sacramento delta and the Colorado River.

Apart from this imported supply of water, Los Angeles is a singular act of will in defiance of nature in a number of other ways. Geologically, it sits upon the grinding edges of two tectonic plates whose surfaces are riven by fault lines that constantly tremble and frequently rupture. I'm reminded of this often, for a spur of the Hollywood Fault runs under our house and I frequently feel the earth shiver underfoot, as if it has goosebumps. In the Northridge quake of January 1994, known locally as the Little Big One, 15,000 brick chimneys toppled across the Southland. The Northridge quake kicked mountains two feet in the air in a matter of seconds and cracked the Los Angeles Basin like an egg in a fist. After that catastrophe, some seismologists suggested the presence of a butterfly-shaped pattern of high stress levels lying under the surface of southern California.

The Southland region is also constantly at risk

from fire. Wind-whipped summer conflagrations spread wings of flame over the Southland's hills and mountains. The gusty Santa Anas fan brush and forest fires, and the dry chaparral burns as though it were soaked with gasoline. Chaparral vegetation has multiple stems growing from a single root crown; its foliage is a dense tinder ripe for sparking. It burns hot—hotter than almost any other kind of natural vegetation, with leaping orange flames that rage through canyons and turn them into chimneys of black smoke. Up to sixteen miles of mountain ridge on the edge of Los Angeles have burned in a single day. In October 1993, brushfires burned from Malibu to Laguna, destroying thousands of homes, displacing people, pets, and wild animals alike.

The Southland is also beset by winter flash floods that cause drastic mud slides and debris flows in its canyons and hillsides. These mud-slicked debris flows can be violent enough to shift boulders the size of automobiles, crushing houses and killing residents in their downhill avalanche.

I can't say that my garden embodies these catastrophic southern California conditions, or even that it much reflects the native flora. On the contrary, the eclectic jumble of plants in my yard comprises an artificial environment, like most of the region's greenery. I've included species from every continent and climate zone, from Asia to Africa, from the alpine to the tropical. My private garden is like Los Angeles in the way it defies its native landscape.

∾

The one way in which my garden does embody the local landscape is in its rocks. It seemed to me that stones would make a more appropriate emblem of the region's character than its native vegetation. After all, it is southern California's unstable geology that looms largest in every Angeleno's consciousness of the surrounding natural forces.

At the same time, stones are ancient symbols of endurance under time's stress. "The rock, the slab, the granite block reveal duration without end," Mircea Eliade observed in *A History of Religious Ideas.* They represent "permanence, incorruptibility—in the last analysis a modality of *existing* independently of temporal becoming."

Because of their enduring strength, stones are also believed to have sexual powers, Eliade noted. In France, right into this century, young Breton peasant women climbed up and slid down granite megaliths in a ritual known as the *glissade.* They hoped that the stones' mythic potency would help them get pregnant.

Since rocks are such icons of power and endurance, I decided to collect them. I hefted sandstone boulders from Mulholland Drive, granite rocks from the Ojai River, crumbly shale slabs from the slopes of the San Gabriel Mountains, and round stones streaked with aplite and gneiss from the Joshua Tree National Monument. On one of my trips to Death Valley I picked up iron red rocks from the peak of Dante's View.

As a symbol of the Pacific Ocean, I scavenged rounded sea stones from El Matador Beach in Malibu. The Pacific can get whipped up by fierce winter storms, and I felt that the ferocity of its watery gods had to be acknowledged and appeased.

Scavenging became a habit. Apart from rocks, I gathered up fallen branches and seedpods from the camphor trees that line my street and stole stop signs and municipal parking notices that had been knocked over by careless cars. I retrieved an old wrought-iron chandelier from one neighbor's garbage and a white pedestal washbasin from another's. I frequented local yard sales, and found such treasures as a dressmaker's cane dummy, a yellow ten-gallon milk can, a pair of white ceramic lions, a cement gargoyle with a ferocious maw, and a couple of plaited straw shrimp traps from Malaysia.

One of my best finds was a carved redwood panel I bought from an aging hippie woodcarver whose workshop bordered one of the Venice canals. That free spirit earned his keep carving fancy front doors featuring mythological beasts for the mansions of Beverly Hills and Bel-Air; in his yard I found a panel with a half-completed dragon he'd abandoned when the wood cracked along a faulty grain.

The dragon attracted me at once. I identified with its emerging presence, which appeared at once half in and half out of the raw redwood. Could the mythical beast come into its own, or would the sheer inertia of its woody origins drag it back into oblivion? I fixed the dragon panel to the fence beside my garden's back gate as a kind of warning to myself.

All these elements added extra layers of narrative detail. Like vivid words or phrases, the stones, driftwood, and other scavenged and collected items enriched the garden's texture. Somehow, they all found places in the greenery without inducing a feeling of clutter. I hung the shrimp traps from an avocado tree branch and draped them with Spanish moss. The dressmaker's cane dummy decorated an ivy-covered trellis, along with the iron chandelier.

The ceramic lions found a shady spot on a corner of the deck.

Out of such stuff I fashioned my first totem pole. The impulse came in response to a feeling that the portal in the middle of my garden was a vacant frame. The late afternoon sun that focused there struck empty air, and this absence nagged at my mind.

Aviva had a foot-high ceramic Buddha she'd bought on a trip to Bali, and it struck me that its plump figure could shine in the rays through the arch. The Buddha would spend most of the day in shadow, until the late sun lit up his smiling face and smooth white bosom. Around the Buddha's neck Aviva hung a religious medallion she'd brought from Thailand's famous Deer Park.

The Buddha sat at the foot of the totem pole, which was formed out of a branch trimmed from the avocado tree. Above the Buddha I put a lifelike plastic snake, sacred to the Greco-Roman god of medicine, Aesculapius, and capped the pole with a black stone owl honoring Minerva, goddess of wisdom. In this way I hoped to invite the protection of a host of mythical powers.

6

Listen and Learn

The new totem pole reinforced a lesson I was slowly learning: If I listened to my garden, it would tell me how it had to grow.

Once established, a garden defines itself, much as a novel creates its own momentum after the basic plot is laid out and the story is set in motion. Just as a writer will falter if he tries to force a narrative in a direction that goes against its grain, so any gardener who does not learn to listen to the voice of his composition will fail.

The gardeners of ancient China recognized this crucial fact. Four thousand years ago they began the history of horticulture by emphasizing natural rhythms lightly touched by a human baton. To orchestrate nature's given harmonies they subtly added the grace notes of pavilions, bridges, gates, steps, and terraces. Listening with an attentive inner ear, the early Chinese gardeners avoided the tone-deaf willfulness that has marked so many human encounters with the landscape.

Such willfulness is epitomized in the work of André Lenôtre, the seventeenth-century French landscapist who imposed a brutal geometric concord upon the garden of the Palace of Versailles. In Lenôtre's designs, the axial vistas of symmetrical parterres, canals, flower beds, fountains, hedges, and allées call to mind the blare and bluster of martial music drowning out the earth's native eloquence.

In a true garden, "every plant is significant and happily used," said Florence Yoch, the doyenne of early southern California's landscapists, who designed the grounds of Tara in Hollywood's production of *Gone with the Wind*.

One day, while sitting quietly in a corner listening to my garden, I thought about the personal, subjective nature of time. In a relatively short period I'd made a garden, a living thing, that seemed eternal. All gardens imply a dimension of eternity, the sense of a world forever in being, yet I'd done all this in a blink of time's eye.

As a child, traveling by train for three days and nights for a thousand miles across the African veld between Bulawayo and Cape Town, where we took our summer vacations, I'd marveled at the way in which the close-up landscape whizzed past while the horizon hardly seemed to move. I could watch the same far-off elephant or giraffe for an hour or more even as the bush sped by under my compartment window.

Time has a similar disjunction. Personal events happen quickly, flashing from one thing to another almost too fast to register, while impersonal events may seem to last forever.

English needs a new tense to encompass this disjunction between personal time and impersonal time, between a particular past and an eternal present. Only such a formulation might allow one to express something of the true human experience of time.

My garden is such a tense to me, compressing a particular past and an eternal future in one small paradisal space.

ॐ

Once I had learned to listen to my garden, to hear the rhythms of its life as well as to take in the symphony of its sounds, smells, and sights, I was rewarded with a fresh wave of inspiration.

The fountains I'd installed demanded their own micro-environments. The water splashing over the rims of the wooden barrels called out for surrounding plants that relished wetness, such as papyrus reeds, horsetail grass, and the small, fragrant oyama magnolias. These in turn suggested the presence of clay pots shaped like swans and ducks, planted with water-loving ferns.

Like the introduction of a new character in a novel, these fountain clusters created yet another layer of narrative in the evolving story of my garden. Their dampness was lush and sexual, rich in decay. Plants rotted quickly in these clammy enclaves, as if consumed by their own lust for life, and the wet soil around the fountains fostered a slimy subworld of slugs, snails, and earthworms.

The water and the worms attracted many birds. Hosts of house wrens and yellow warblers gathered to drink and gossip on the lip of the cherub fountain's bowl, while robins and finches hopped around the barrels, plucking at earthworms. Cedar wax-wings twittered in the jessamine branches, pausing to drink between greedy beakfuls of white berries. Hummingbirds made a bidet of the water jetting from the fish's mouth, riding the wet curve with their tails spread, and a pair of crows strolled the paths like cops on the beat, poking their beaks into everybody's business.

Sometimes I had difficulty interpreting the garden's voices. For instance, I knew the potted shrimp plant I'd located in the shade of the solanum shrub was in the wrong place. The justicia's delicate white and coppery bronze flowers were paled by comparison with the solanum's intense purple blooms; they called out to be moved to another spot—but where?

I tried the shrimp plant under the bougainvillea canopy at the rear of the garden, but the shade was too dense, and its flowers drooped. I moved it to a place beside the archway, but its delicacy was lost against the busy background of the climbing ivy and the trumpet vine. I humped that heavy pot to six different locations before it came to rest beside the fish fountain, where it immediately flourished. The shrimplike spikes glistened in the light, damp shade, and the leaves grew bushy. When the flowers turned black I pinched them off and let them fall to decay and enrich the wet surrounding ground.

Yet other lessons I learned from the garden concerned the uses of decay and the purpose of catastrophe.

Decaying plants and rotting leaves not only gave their stored energy back to the soil, but they also embodied the fact of death. Along with the small corpses of bumblebees, wasps, moths, and butterflies common in every garden, rotting vegetation served as a reminder of the slow entropy that is integral to all natural systems.

Catastrophe, too, has its vital purpose. "Examine the lives of the best and most fruitful men and peoples," Nietzsche wrote in *The Gay Science*, "and ask yourselves whether a tree, if it is to grow proudly into the sky, can do without bad weather or storms."

The truth of Nietzsche's words became evident in my garden when wild winds snapped a heavy avocado branch, which fell and smashed all the plants beneath. My heart sank when I first viewed the wreckage. Then I realized that the disaster was also an opportunity. The foliage the branch had crushed was boring, and now I could reshape it to a better presence, a more favoring circumstance.

What the spot called out for was another totem pole. I put a sturdy redwood post in the ground and decorated it with some Mexican clay wall pots. I capped the pole with the cane dressmaker's dummy and the curlicued wrought-iron chandelier that I moved from their original position on the ivy trellis, and draped them with a spray of bougainvillea. The effect was slightly sinister, resembling a cannibal's stake topped by a torso and a shrunken head, an image that conjured up Kurtz's compound in Conrad's *Heart of Darkness*. Aviva protested that all this totemic stuff verged on voodoo.

Another kind of catastrophe was created by my next-door neighbor's decision to rip out his backyard to put in a swimming pool. Early one morning my ears were deafened by the roar of a bulldozer tearing up his garden. I watched in horror as the machine's brutal yellow bucket sucked up the splendid red bougainvillea that covered my neighbor's garage roof.

Witnessing this rampage, I realized that my neighbor's vast and colorful bougainvillea and his ruby-fruited persimmon tree had formed a backdrop above my north garden fence. Now that horizon seemed naked and exposed, open to the raw sky.

After the first shock, I responded vigorously. I added a four-foot trellis atop the six-foot white board fence that separated my property from my neighbor's. Then I planted a row of rapid-growing Cape honeysuckle vines I knew would soon make a thick green web over the fence and trellis.

For good measure, I put in a wisteria vine. Its violet-purple bloom clusters recalled the Molyvos agora I described in *Dreaming of You*, roofed over by a similar wisteria. In spring, after a storm, the village cobbles were covered in fallen flowers; in summer the wisteria's green shade dappled the outdoor cafe tables along the sloping avenue; in winter the ancient vine's bare branches let the pale sunlight through to warm the shopfronts.

Winter storms were dramatic in the Spanish village of Altea, where I lived for five years with my young family in the late 1950s and early '60s. Winds drove billowing baroque clouds across the dome of heaven toward some distant thunder while rain fell in slashes that knifed their way through our villa's old Roman tile roof. The wild air shook the ancient olive trees, scattering fruit black as goat droppings, and the flowering almond trees carpeted rocky terraces with pink and white foam. White narcissi, bent flat, filled the air with a lemony sweetness.

These storms were followed by periods of brilliant clarity. In the bright moonlight salamanders ran across the white wall that served as the screen for the summer outdoor cinema, pausing to rest in the melon eye of Sophia Loren or on the edge of George Raft's glistening spats. At dusk the colors of the dying sun reflected in the sea shimmered with ultramarine, apple green, and cobalt, fading to violet, then purple, and finally to charcoal while the departing sardine boats sailed away like tin cutouts against the sky.

On one such golden day in Altea following a storm, we celebrated my daughter Karen's fourth birthday. Celestina, a local widow, agreed to make a huge *paella con todo* over a cane fire and serve it to our friends under the pergola beside her white-washed house.

The paella's main ingredient was a plump white rabbit, which Celestina killed and skinned before our eyes. She took the animal by the ears and held it up high. The rabbit jerked its hind legs for a while before accepting its fate. Its furry belly, fattened for the feast, was exposed to the sunlight sifting through the pergola vine.

Celestina's clothes were so old they'd taken on a mother-of-pearl sheen. Her round peasant face, marked with hard lines (though she was only in her early forties), was turned away from the dangling rabbit as if she'd momentarily forgotten it was in her fist.

My daughter huddled against my trouser leg, transfixed with terror at the creature's plight. "Tell her to stop," she sobbed. When I conveyed this tearful plea to the widow she merely shrugged, dismissing our sentimentality. Taking aim with the edge of her palm, she delivered a swift karate chop to the base of the rabbit's skull. The animal let out a

99

childlike scream, and collapsed. Celestina smiled and said: *"La vida es un soplo y hay que soplarla,"* which, loosely translated, means, Life is but a breath to be sighed.

Karen stared with horrified fascination at the sight of the beast now dumped on the tiles like a loose bag of fur. "Will I be dead one day?" she asked.

While Celestina cooked the paella in the open air over the crackling canes, we drank a raw red rioja and nibbled roasted sparrows rolled in honey. The paella's odors, rich with rabbit, calamari, shrimp, red peppers, french beans, clams, mussels, and juicy chunks of pork, charged our nostrils and made us ravenous. The fragrance of the cooking saffron rice filled the hot noon air, mingling with the raunchy odor of the goats in Celestina's pen.

The smells drove our dog mad. Moro was a local black mongrel who'd taught himself to dance to amuse the foreigners and gain their sympathy, thereby rescuing himself from the desperation of the pack of starving dogs that haunted the fields on the outskirts of town. Excited by the prospect of some juicy bones, this "self-made dog," as we called him, pranced around the pan on his hind legs, slavering.

We drank wine from leather *botijos*, squirting the crimson stream into our mouths. Karen and my seven-year-old son, Paul, were allowed sips, and they, like the rest of us, were soon pleasantly tiddly. After we had our fill of the paella, grabbing portions from the pan with our fingers, Karen seemed reconciled to the rabbit's fate. She contentedly rubbed her plump tummy against one of the poles supporting the pergola, murmuring into the ragged ear of her teddy bear, Zoozie.

After the dish was wolfed down to the last scrap of yellow rice, we striped one another's faces with carbon from the underside of the pan to bring good luck, according to the local tradition. As the low, late sun drifted behind Celestina's cottage we sleepily laid down on the warm tiles, licking our greasy lips.

One summer afternoon a few weeks later I took Paul to see a bullfight in a neighboring town. The program was a *novillada* featuring novice matadors out to make their mark, usually by taking risks their more established elders were too wise and wary to attempt.

Paul and I arrived early at the *plaza de toros*, and found seats over the *arrastre*, the tunnel under the stands through which both the bullfighters and the bull enter the ring. Our legs dangled over the tunnel, so we could look down between our knees upon the heads of the emerging picadors on their horses.

Then, as the band played the traditional *paso dobles*, the trumpeting music that heightens everyone's pulse, the young bull charged out below us. The warmth of its black body and agitated breath, the musky smell of its animal rage rose up to us in a hot wave. Paul let out a strangled shriek and grabbed my arm, frightened by the force of the bull's fury.

Because it was a *novillada*, the picadors went easy on the bull. They dug their long lances into the animal's powerful neck muscles perfunctorily while the animal tried out its sharp horns on their mounts' padded flanks. After the pics, the *banderilleros* jabbed their streamer-decorated barbs into the bull's neck wounds to enrage it further and get it to carry its head low enough for the matador to go in over the horns for the kill.

With the lowering sun in our eyes, the crowd screaming *"Toro! Toro! Toro!"* and the brassy music of the band pounding in our ears, the smell of blood and sand in our noses, Paul and I were drunk with excitement. We clung close and sweating while watching the dance of the young matador as he leaned in close with his crimson cape—much too close—and all but invited the bull to jab his horns through the glitter of his gaudy suit of lights. When the final sword went in over the beast's exhausted head and vanished between its shoulder blades, a mighty roar rose up from the spectators. I heard myself roaring, too, and turned to see Paul's young face hot with delirious delight.

The carcass was harnessed to a team of horses and dragged out of the arena through the tunnel beneath our feet. In death, deserted by its violence, the bull was nothing but a collapsed bag of black skin. The dark blood oozing from its back left a dirty trail in the dust as the young *novillero* ran around the ring, waving the beast's severed ears at the crowd.

On the bus ride home Paul was silent. His eyes were big with amazement. When, finally, I asked him what he thought of his first *corrida*, he paused a long moment, then said: "What happened to the bull?" I explained that it was immediately butchered; its meat would be sold off to eager buyers while its horns and tail were turned into wall ornaments. The boy began to cry.

Listening to my garden taught me to cock an ear for the internal pulse of the narrative growing in my typewriter. Whenever I tried to push the story in ways counter to its inherent thrust, I was bothered by the same unease that would trouble me whenever I attempted to impose a false pattern on the plants in my yard. A small voice pricked my conscience and led me back to the organic flow.

Alternating between the novel flourishing in my Selectric and the story blooming in my garden, I began to see how interchangeable the two were, taken as metaphors. If a garden could be thought of as a green novel, a novel might be imagined as a white garden, words planted on the page.

To follow a passage of Proust, say, is to meander like a drowsy bee through a lavish cultivation, thickening the pollen of memory with the nectar of rumination in dreamy, lingering paragraphs. Perusing any long sentence in *The Guermantes Way*, for example, you can sniff the trace of eternity wafting through the air in the smell of hawthorn blossom in Proust's Combray.

Henry James's word-gardens offer a more tangled visit. James's sentences seem constantly threatened by thought-weeds, as though the sensuality of their verbal vegetation were fraught with a deep distrust of all things natural. In *The Wings of a Dove*, for instance, Milly Theale's "tragic, pathetic, ironic, these indeed for the most part sinister, liabilities" must be defended against the unruly undergrowth haunting the ordered terraces of "the general perfect taste."

Dickens's word-gardens, on the other hand, glory in their weeds. The Dickensian undergrowth is vigorous and vivid, charged with a lush and demonic life force that seems far more real than the pale blooms of goodness he cultivates like roses on a dungheap. Going one better than Dickens, Dostoevsky grows a dense, dark word-jungle in which the dazed reader stumbles over roots of pain that can twist an ankle, snap a knee, or break a heart.

No word-garden is more choked with weeds or more marshy than Louis-Ferdinand Céline's. In Céline's patch it is hell's season all year round; the stench of rot is everywhere, and everything human is Satan's mulch. His fetid prose crashes through thickets of terror in a Garden of Earthly Frights. The shotgun suicide of the mad genius-inventor des Pereires in *Death on the Installment Plan* is presented in brutal verbiage punctuated by airy dots: "The double barrel went in through his mouth and passed straight through his head...It was like hash on a skewer...shreds, chunks, and sauce...Big blood clots, patches of hair...He had no eyes at all...They'd blown out..."

For relief, hurry to James Joyce's jolly pages. Here a jig-a-jig phrasiculturalist crossbreeds weeds and orchids to create marvelous blooms of tonguage. In the luxuriant word-beds of *Finnegans Wake* you find "The horn for breakfast, one o'going for lunch and dinnerchime. As popular as when Belly the First was keng and his members met in the Diet of Man."

After dancing through such plump Irish greenery, look for the lean drought of Cervantes's cactus garden where prickly nobilities grace stony pathways. "Ours is beyond doubt the more laborious and arduous calling, the more beset by hunger and thirst, more wretched, ragged and ridden with lice," says toothless old Don Quixote jogging along on his rawboned nag. "Thus we become the ministers of God on earth, and our arms the means by which he executes His decrees."

7

Fungus, Rot, and Mildew

As the spring of 1989 passed into summer, something odd and very disturbing began to happen in my own word-garden: *Dreaming of You* sank into a marsh.

It happened suddenly. The ground of text, which had been firm and hard underfoot, abruptly turned soggy. One moment I was walking on a solid surface, the next I was up to my chest in verbal slush.

The contrast between the garden's vigor and the miasma rotting the phrases I planted on my pages made me desperate. And while gardening filled me with energy, writing sucked at my soul. After a session at my Selectric I felt wrung out, limp as a rag; words exhausted my body and mind. On the other hand, the hours I spent digging, planting, hoeing, transplanting, mulching, deadheading, watering, fertilizing, pruning, and raking gave my aching muscles a gift of pleasure and a flowing sense of achievement.

As the days passed I spent less and less time with words. Resting in the shade after hours of good hard gardening, I agonized over my novel's lapse, the apparent failure of its will to live. Its core energy seemed to have drained away, like a shrub whose roots have rotted. There were several possible explanations, but in the end the true reason why my book had wilted eluded me.

My now lifeless words echoed the mysterious contrasts in vitality apparent in the plant world. Just as the sap pushes through a plant's stem, manifesting itself in leaves, seeds, and flowers, so the mind's energy is expressed in images and verbal growth. Both sap and mind may flourish or fail for strange reasons of their own, so that nature comes through pure and powerful in some specimens, corrupted and weak in others.

Was there, then, a connection between these variations in vegetative power and the faltering force of my mind manifested in the rot, fungus, and mildew withering the pages of *Dreaming of You*?

As with my words, it was a puzzle why some species thrived mightily while others failed. Why were morning glories, say, so unstoppably vigorous while the roses dropped, despite all my tender loving care? What was the nature of the crude energy that spread the ignored bougainvillea and failed the cosseted gardenias? Why did the lantana sprout its charming miniature bouquets, exuding tangy odors, while the azaleas seemed always to hover on the edge of extinction? And even within the same species, some plants flourished while others flagged.

Did these disparities serve secret purposes of survival and decay? If so, the failure of my words might have secret strategies of its own, allowing the rot of old notions, the dissolution of exhausted ways of being. If that was the case, I decided, the best thing for me to do just then was to leave words alone and simply cultivate my garden, hoping to be soothed by its deep harmonies.

♠

My friend Bernie, an American journalist in the London bureau of a major U.S. metropolitan daily, had a theory about such harmonies. He explained it to me one afternoon in the summer of 1964 as we walked across the misty meadows along the Thames near Cookham, the hamlet in the Berkshire countryside west of London made famous by the painter Stanley Spencer.

Cookham Village and this stretch of the river figure in many of Spencer's canvases, especially those that fuse local scenes with biblical events. Spencer's

Last Supper, for instance, shows Christ and the Apostles with their bare toes tucked under the table of a village malt house. His *Resurrection* takes place in the Cookham cemetery, while the local dead look on in wonder. "During the morning I am visited and walk about in that visitation," Spencer wrote of his life in Cookham. "I leave off at dusk, delighted with the spiritual work I have done."

Bernie and I were spending a weekend in Cookham, staying at a pub on the Thames not far from the converted chapel where Spencer painted, which now houses some of his canvases and sketches. From breakfast to bedtime we walked up and down the riverbank, heatedly discussing everything, including Marxism and Judaism, architecture and poetry, America and England. Our passionate argument—his passion, my argument—continued through riverside lunches and pints of warm bitter ale, and on through evenings before the tavern's log fire.

"The Kabbalist doctrine of *tikkun*, 'the restoration of the sparks,' concerns the recreation of an original, shattered harmony," Bernie explained one morning as we tramped across the rich green English grass still wet with dew. "When Adam was expelled from Eden his great spirit exploded, scattering a shower of divine sparks upon all the souls waiting to be born. Each man's job is to restore that primal harmony by redeeming the spark from the mud of our minds and the ugliness of our spirits."

I could see that conflict between mind-mud and the divine spark writ plain in Bernie's skinny frame. The emotional fervor of his intellect, spurting forth in staccato bursts of breath, seemed to have twisted his body, skewing it out of shape like a blasted tree trunk. His face was pocked with a scattershot of old acne craters, his teeth were yellowed with neglect, the corners of his mouth were often stained with whitish spittle—but his eyes were sharp brown chips of pure intelligence. In his company I was often groggy with talk and beer, elated at the rush of ideas he poured forth in such passionate profusion.

One afternoon after our country tramp we rested on Cookham Bridge, leaning our elbows on the metal parapet. The Thames is narrow in its upper reaches, and Cookham Bridge is a simple steel span springing from bank to bank.

"I must have a bridge or I can't think," Bernie said. In his time, he went on, he'd leaned on the parapets of Paris's Pont des Arts, Florence's Ponte Vecchio, Venice's Bridge of Sighs, San Francisco's Golden Gate, Detroit's Ambassador; on the balustrades of canal bridges in Amsterdam, over the Guadalquivir in Seville, over the Tagus in Toledo, over the Rhine, the Danube, the Euphrates, the Menander, the Tiber, the Po, the Volga, the Indus, and the Yellow River.

"There's this story," Bernie said as we watched the summer swans float by below. "About a man named George." He shifted from one foot to another, adjusting his bony elbows on the bridge rail. His voice was soft, almost caressing under the flat Brooklyn vowels.

"George was clean in body and mind. Each morning he put on his bowler and took the train from Welwyn Garden Suburb to the City of London, along with all the other nice penguins perched in rows behind their *Times* and *Daily Telegraph*s.

"Like his colleagues, George had a wife and daughter and a garden. Sadly, though, his wife died one day and there was only the daughter and the garden. George didn't mind too much. He loved the girl to distraction. She was a looker, his Jenny. He nurtured, fussed, and tended her with all the tenderness and strangled passion his very private English heart could conjure, which is a very great deal.

"Jenny grew clean and bright and lovely as the mums lining George's garden path. He watched her adoringly when she brought him his evening tea when he got home and sat before the grate in his woolly slippers. Every gesture, every movement she made was magical to George. Jenny was the only thing that made his life worth a damn.

"Their intimacy was a delight beyond imagining, almost beyond bearing. The lovelier she became, the more he was tormented by her grace, her selfless devotion to daddy, her—to him—more than human beauty in a world he knew was nothing but a pile of crap. On Jenny's seventeenth birthday, after they'd blown out the candle and cut the chocolate cake she'd baked, George stabbed his daughter to death."

Bernie paused, cleared his throat, and continued. "The coroner counted seventeen separate stab wounds on the girl's body—one for each birthday. The police were amazed. 'Why did you assault her so many times, old chap?' the kindly Detective Inspector asked. 'I mean to say, seventeen times! Isn't that a trifle, well, excessive?'

"George didn't answer. In fact, he didn't say another word, not even when he was sentenced to detention at Her Majesty's pleasure in Broadmoor, the prison for the criminally insane. One reporter in the yellow press, more perceptive than most scribblers, labeled George's murderous attack on Jenny an 'act of total love.' Inspired by the madness of it all, he suggested that 'when a man loves too much he instinctively reaches for the knife, to slice through the veils of illusion to touch another's heart.'"

"Oh my gawd," I said. "That's some story!"

"It happened." He threw back his head, flung out his arms, and recited George Herbert's lines that begin:

Oh England! full of sin, but most of sloth,
Spit out thy phlegm, and fill thy breast with glory:
Thy gentry bleats, as if thy native cloth
Transfused a sheepishness into thy story.

Three years later, after returning to Manhattan, Bernie cut off all contact with me. He had tried to convince me that my marriage to Janine was a futility; I knew he was right, but at the time I just couldn't bring myself to leave her. Maybe the sheepishness that transfused *my* story in those years finally bored him.

୨ର

One morning I took the manuscript of *Dreaming* into the garden and placed it on a small pile of dead leaves. Whatever the cause, it was increasingly clear that the book had died on the vine and should be decently done away with. I put a match to the pile and watched it burn. As the pages went up in a puff of smoke I felt as light as air myself, released from a dead weight. But there was a bitter aftertaste of failure to this ceremony.

A few weeks later I resigned from the *Herald-Examiner*. This action was prompted by the presence of a new associate editor, an alcoholic bully who told me right off the bat that architecture was "irrelevant to a hard-news daily." Not long after my resignation, at the end of 1989, the paper itself folded, put down by its owner, the Hearst Corporation, like a mangy old dog that could no longer wag its tail.

Leaving my job and burning my manuscript left me with little to do. I felt as if I were sinking in the same swamp that had swallowed my novel. I moped through the whole winter, and on into early spring. In February, Aviva went away for six weeks to visit family and friends in Canada. In my glum mood I felt abandoned, and slowly the black mud of self-pity sucked me right under.

The garden became my bolt-hole. I wanted to dig myself deep into its warm black soil like an earthworm, draw the ground up over my head, and never see the sun again. Hidden in the garden, vulnerable to fears nameable and unnameable, I lived a wholly underground existence. It was a strange experience, frightening and unbearable, charged with unwelcome, unhappy memories that suddenly blossomed in my mind.

Buried in the garden's deep, dank folds I remembered that the dream landscape of Molyvos was also the place where my first marriage had collapsed...

In the early 1970s Janine and I went to Molyvos to try to mend our cracking connection. We arrived in Lesbos with the February storms, and in our whitewashed house high up on the hill we could watch the bay switch moods from black-browed fury to halcyon sunlit seascapes. In the morning, clouds dark with rage sat low on the horizon's head and winds wrenched at our closed shutters. Later, low evening shafts of sun turned the underbellies of those clouds to gold. In a scene out of a rococo mural, fat and joyful cherubs seemed to sing from heaven on that first day of Creation when the Lord said, "Let there be light."

But as the Greek summer wore on, as the baking earth and sky turned to bleached tones of brown and blue, Janine and I discovered yet again how truly sad we were, separately and with one another. Our mutual misery coiled itself into a rope that became the last bond tying us to a common shore. "Nothing's quite as engrossing as a really bad marriage," Janine remarked sardonically.

For distraction, I took long, solitary walks across the fields and up the hills behind the town. The burnt summer landscape gave off a smell of baking earth. Crested hoopoes mocked me from the olive trees, and nanny goats snickered as I passed. My head buzzed with an endless interior dialogue in which I argued with Janine over the corpse of our marriage. The busy thoughts were like a swarm of flies feeding on the carcass of my years with a woman whom I should have loved, had tried to love, but couldn't.

Finally, we split up and Janine left Molyvos. I went crazy for a while. Isolated on a remote island in the middle of winter, I plunged into a black pool of melancholy during the lonely, windswept months.

The Greeks were miserable, too. In the taverns the jolly songs of summer switched to mournful dirges. The local fishermen, fueled by ouzo and retsina, smashed plates in a hysterical frenzy. Young soldiers posted far from home danced on cafe tabletops, and a bridegroom put his fist through a window after the wedding ceremony, spraying his screaming bride's white gown with blood from his slashed arm.

Imitating these purgative frenzies, I danced and drank with the most berserk Molyvotes. But I'm no Greek. After such mad revels I felt exhausted and empty, with only the thought of suicide to see me through many a bad night in that long, hard time.

This, then, was the truth about the personal emotional landscape I had tried to render as a place to dream. No wonder I'd failed so miserably.

❧

Back in my garden, I began to revive. My revival was charged by a rising anger, which seemed to generate itself in my stomach. The fresh energy of this gut rage was a force in its own right, shoving aside the inertia that had driven me so deep into the marshland of my spirit.

Although I had been moping in the garden, I'd been too self-absorbed to care for the plants and the yard had gone wild. The vines, bushes, and shrubs were so dense and entwined that the coherence of the place had been lost in a green blur. Like me, the garden had temporarily lost its definition and direction.

Leaping to the attack, wielding clippers and shears, I chopped back the vines and sliced away tangled tendrils of bougainvillea, trumpet vine, jasmine, and abutilon. Without mercy, I ripped out azaleas, gardenias, begonias, hydrangeas, clematis, canna lilies, pavonias, red ginger, and every other green growing thing that appeared to be less than one hundred percent alive and charged with vigor.

The fierce pleasure I found in this frenzy differed from the bitter joy I'd felt when burning *Dreaming*. Both were acts of creative destruction, but where the novel had been reduced to nothing but a pile of ashes, the garden would put out new growth—an advantage vegetation has over verbiage.

True, there were devastated patches here and there where I'd pruned the foliage to the quick. The trumpet vine over the archway looked as if a crazy barber had run riot, leaving it bald. The morning glory was stripped down to loose strands, like an old man's last few wispy locks. The area around the dolphin fountain was cleared, shaven to the scalp of the bare wet ground.

In the end, I was delighted to see that my assault had given the garden a fresh transparency. Cutting back the greenery had opened the whole yard to the light. Through the thinned-out canopy of bougainvillea I could now view the delicate yet gaudy pink flowers of the silk floss tree beside the back fence. The pruned branches of the pencil tree revealed the skinny stems and floating leaves of the young Hong Kong orchid tree. A chrome yellow hibiscus, once smothered under a blanket of jasmine, began to bloom for the first time; a bird of paradise bush put out plumes like a rooster raising his coxcomb. All in all, the green power of the garden seemed more lucid than ever.

The surge of new energy that flowed through me and my garden was epitomized by the blossoming of a coral tree I had planted two years earlier, a tree I'd thought would never flower. Now, suddenly, the coral lit up a sunny corner, its carmine candles glowing with an inner fire.

As I marveled at this sight, I recalled the coral tree that dominated the dusty compound of my Uncle Abe's store at Marula, in the Matabeleland country-side outside Bulawayo. Known locally as a *kaffir-boom*—Afrikaans for "nigger-tree," so named because the Africans used it for firewood—the coral dropped its leaves in spring and became a scrawny icon in the bush, graced by honey-dripping bloom clusters.

120

Marula was a one-horse watering stop for the trains that ran south to Mafeking. My uncle's general store beside the tracks serviced a largely African clientele with everything from corn meal and lamp paraffin to the colored beads and trinkets that supposedly fascinated all "savages." The store's tin-roofed verandah was a local meeting place, always crowded with noisy young men and women, with mothers carrying babies strapped to their backs and kids wearing nothing but drawstring Tom Thumb tobacco pouches as codpieces.

The radio played loudly all the time, mostly American swing and Shaftesbury Avenue show tunes. The racket was counterpointed by the click and clatter of Ndebele and the curses of my highly irritable relative, who despised with a passion the *schwartzes* who provided him with a comfortable living.

I was in Marula the Sunday morning in September 1939, when the Second World War broke out. The music stopped abruptly and King George VI's frail voice, declaring from distant London that we were at war with Germany, warned, "There may be dark days ahead."

The listening Africans were both awed and elated at hearing the sovereign's voice; when the king's short speech was over they applauded vociferously.

My Uncle Abe's response was very different. "Oy, we'll suffer," he moaned. "Like the Jews in Germany."

"Us?" I gulped, my eight-year-old heart squeezed by fear.

My uncle was in shock; his watery eyes reflected a ghetto Jew's fear of terrible events. He reacted from this old instinct, though all his life he'd lived a perfectly protected existence in Rhodesia, tainted only by the snobbery and social anti-Semitism of the English colonials.

The ancient terror in my uncle's eyes turned my knees to jelly. In a panic, I fled out of the store and ran as fast as my young legs would carry me, as far from that terrible threat as I could get.

Breathless, I leaned against an acacia and watched an engine taking on water. An elephantlike trunk reached down from the elevated tank tower, squirting thousands of gallons to cool the locomotive's belly. The fireman perched on top of the engine to steady the canvas hose was silhouetted against a wide sky bleached white by the sun.

When I got my breath back I walked away into the bush, squinting my eyes in the blazing light. Soon all signs of civilization vanished and the barren grassland was relieved only by an occasional thorn-tree twisting its bare, knotty branches in what seemed like hopeless prayer. The ground was so hot it burned my soles through my tennis shoes. I felt as though I were wrapped in a ball of fire. Even my eyeballs were on fire, spurting flames into my brain.

Then an amazing, unexpected feeling of safety came over me. For reasons I couldn't define, I felt secure within Africa's hot heart, as if the heat in my body and the sun in the blazing sky had fused to scorch away my fright.

∾

Decades later, I felt the same sense of deep security in my decimated garden, but this time the reasons were clear to me. On the one hand, the uncontrolled violence I'd let loose on the garden's body had proved that I could do my absolute worst and still not destroy its essential structure and regenerative power. On the other hand, my energetic outburst had drained away my fears and left me feeling as if my bones were stripped clean.

This newfound feeling of safety was so delicious that I took to sleeping in the garden. I set a camp bed under the bougainvillea canopy and drifted off with the sweet smell of spring-blooming night jessamine in my nose and the splash of fountains soothing my ears.

One night I dreamed of being ten years old, buying watermelons in the market with my maternal grandfather...

It's a little ritual we've established, he and I; every Friday during the annual summer visits my mother and I make to Bloemfontein in the Orange Free State, Grandpa takes me to the central market to buy watermelons.

He's an expert at telling which melons are ripe, he says. But then, he's an expert at everything. When he pronounces an opinion, his argumentative sons and daughters fall silent, cowed by his stubbornness and his bullying tone, and maybe by memories of the painful beatings he inflicted when they were children.

The *sjambok* rawhide whip with which he enforced family discipline still hangs behind the kitchen door. To my child's eyes its black leather seems darkened with old bloodstains, relics of the lashings my mother has described. She has a long, faint scar on her shoulder that makes me shudder every time I see it.

Grandpa is frightening in many ways. His fierce

religiosity gives him the air of a biblical character, more like one of Pharoah's brutal overseers than any child of Israel. His rough Russian Yiddish–accented growl, reinforced by bristly jowls, gives him the aspect of a wild and foreign beast. To top it all, his stiff suit, worn to a shine and infused with the stale pungency of mothballs, exudes an alien smell mixed with the aroma of the cabbage soup he downs by the bowl. To me, he's a being from another planet, and snippets of adult conversations I overhear compound the strangeness.

I hear that he was a master baker in Kiev; that he abandoned the family for six years to return to a mistress he'd left behind in the Ukraine; and that on his return he fathered Pearl, my youngest aunt, even though my grandmother was totally paralyzed with rheumatoid arthritis.

I know he cheats at chess. When I'm not looking, he moves the pieces, then threatens me with dire punishment when I protest. Once he brandished the dreaded *sjambok* in my face, and that led to a heated confrontation between Grandpa and my mother in which she threatened to murder him if he touched me.

Bloemfontein was the heart of pro-Nazi Afrikanerdom. In the midst of the war against Hitler, Nazi mobs roamed the city beating up Jews. On one occasion my eccentric Uncle Alec was cornered by a gang of thugs who broke his arm. Another time, when we were shopping in a downtown department store, my mother slapped the face of a fat farmer who called her a "Jew bitch."

The sound that slap made, like the bursting of a paper bag, haunted me for years; the look of absolute ferocity on my mother's face frightened me as much as it did her victim.

But in the market, all these murky overtones vanish. Acres of fruit stalls stretch away into the dim distance of the tin-roofed hall. The watermelons alone, piled high like fat bombs, fill several aisles, scenting the morning with their crisp green smell.

Grandpa tests every melon with the air of a physician listening to heartbeats, cocking an ear to hear the echo his tapping fingers generates within each fruit. If, as he explains for the hundredth time, the echo gives back what he calls an "avantilation"—his made-up word for a certain hollow resonance—the melon is ripe. He ignores the exhortations of the Hindu vendors and distrusts the skilfully sliced sample triangles they offer for his taste. "The ear is not a fool," he says, over and over. "Always the ear. Listen for the avantilation."

Finally, after testing dozens, he makes his choice. The selected melon is then weighed and the price is haggled over passionately. Grandpa's guttural contempt punctuates the vendor's singsong Gujerati protestations.

Pennies are divided into ha'pennies and down to farthings as the bargaining is refined. The total cost of the ten-pound watermelon is settled at one shilling and fivepence three-farthings, and grandpa is triumphant. "We made a bargain," he crows. "This is a very fine melon." I stagger under the weight of the prize he's grandly handed me to carry, awed by his arrogance.

After the market comes the real treat: a visit to the Plaza cafe-bioscope. In this cinema meals are served, to be guzzled in the dark while watching a continuous reel of cartoons, serials, and shorts. While the Three Stooges shove cream pies in one another's face and Zorro flourishes his whip—a spine-tingling reminder of Grandpa's *sjambok*—he and I down plates of the spicy Malay curry called *baboetie* balanced on trays attached to the row of seats in front.

Stomach bulging replete, I lean back in my seat and watch the scratchy screen. Grandpa's profile, glimpsed in the flickering light, seems even more alien than usual. I wonder, Is this man really my mother's father? Can this strange old man's blood run in *my* veins?

In the dawn, looking up at the bright sky through a veil of leaves in the good green place I had made, I wondered why I'd ever been sad or desperate. The vigor of plants, their powerful will to grow and thrive, seemed utterly at odds with my all-too-human tendency to shrivel and wilt.

I lay still for a long time watching the heavens lighten, feeling I'd come to rest in the navel of the world. In the early morning quietness I fancied I could hear the echo of that original Eden in which human beings were as rooted in the powers of the earth as any tree or flower.

When Aviva came home a week later, I hugged her hard, delighted to have her back. She was the real Eve in my Eden, and my world was complete.

8

Restorations

In my recent fury I had pruned, uprooted, chopped, and ripped the garden. Now it was time to make amends, to restore and nurture, to tend the plants with affection.

I healed the baldest spots first, such as the area around the fish fountain I'd laid bare. I surrounded the wooden water barrel with Mexican ferns with long leaves like torn paper, an Australian tree fern unfolding scrolls of foliage, Fijian ferns uncurling coiled tongues of delicate tracery, and several asparagus ferns, some dense, others light and lacy. I planted another osmanthus bush for the subtle sweetness of its scent, and added a downy damask rose whose arching canes dropped pink petals into the water barrel.

Across from the fish fountain, at the top of the steps leading down from the main deck, I arranged a cluster of pots with vivid accents of color. Yellow spikes of verbascum jostled with the soft lavender-purple blooms of leafy ruellia and the bristly bracts of a pineapple lily. At the foot of the steps I planted a saucer-flowered magnolia bush with fragrant white blooms. Beside that I put a dwarf fig tree, pruned like a bonsai, for the shape of its leaves and the ripe sexual smell of its fruit.

I planted a sinewy snail vine on a trellis and watched it put out violet flowers from its crustacean calyx shells. The snail vine shared the trellis with a lavender clematis whose blooms opened like palms offered for reading. Nearby, I hung a Costa Rican nightshade vine in a wooden planter for the contrast of its prickly stems and clusters of lilac blue, yellow-stamened blossoms. I elaborated this corner with the light chartreuse flowers of Corsican hellebore, the singed orange flowers of *Ruttya frutescens*, and pots of delicately scented, pink-throated winter daphne.

Throughout the garden I added a host of such details, creating a more refined texture of leaf and flower without compromising its essential vigor. The new flowers, vines, and shrubs I planted were more finely textured than most of the earlier vegetation, more particular and elegant in shape and surface.

Such refinement required a basis of good health, a sound body wisely nourished. Following old garden lore, I kept my coffee grounds and tea leaves to sprinkle around the roots of acid-loving azaleas, gardenias, and camellias. I fed the ferns ripe bananas and buried the peels to add their potassium-rich humus to the soil. I spaded a mix of chopped apple and pear cores into the earth around the solanum and put rusty iron nails into the ground near the hydrangeas to turn their blossoms blue.

Every day, in the early morning and at dusk, I patrolled the garden, alert for any plant requiring attention. I watered each one individually to ensure it had the right amount of moisture, delivered in a spray, sprinkle, or stream. I washed the leaves with the hose, cleaning away the city grime that settled there like the film on a drunk's tongue, and deadheaded old flowers as soon as they wilted.

Once again I enjoyed finding the right context for each plant in the garden's narrative, discovering by intuition and by trial and error where each bush or shrub had its best place in the green sequence.

For example, I had set a sago palm in a red clay pot shaped like a miniature burro amidst a bank of shrubbery. I hadn't noticed until now that its perkiness was lost in all that foliage; it needed to be singled out, situated in sunlight, featured as a detail and not diminished as a mere incident among a host of less vivid paragraphs of greenery.

I shifted the sago burro to the left of the archway in the center of the garden. Here the afternoon sun lit up its cheerful muzzle and brought out the glossy texture of the palm fronds sprouting from its back. With this move, many of the surrounding plants seemed to take on a fresh glow, illuminated by the richness of this new detail.

At the rear of the garden's last chamber I constructed a jagged redbrick wall five feet high, meant to simulate a ruin. I wanted to add that note to my garden as a reminder of my recent emotional collapse, and my survival.

By inference, too, the broken brick wall was an image expressing the cycle of decline and renewal inherent in all human landscapes. As Schiller wrote in *William Tell,*

> What's old collapses, times change,
> And new life blossoms in the ruins.

New life was blossoming, too, in the ruins of my confidence as a writer. My nurturing fostered the yard's regeneration; in turn, the garden's new growth recharged my courage. I helped it live and it helped me live, and I began to write another novel.

The creative energy flowed both ways. Without my daily attentions, the garden would have lost its distinction and its definition, would quickly become ragged and unkempt. Without the garden's boundless vigor to inspire me, I couldn't have continued to sprout words, and my soul would soon have gone to seed.

Soon thoughts of gardening and thoughts of writing were entwined again like twin vines flourishing day and night in my head. Each night before I dropped off to sleep I reviewed the day's gardening, remembering the new plants I had put in the ground, the shrubs pruned, the bushes staked and fertilized. In this nocturnal recollection I created a mental garden to match the one in my backyard, imprinting the garden on my spirit just as my spirit was imprinted on the garden.

'*Les parfums, les couleurs et les sons se répondent*,' Baudelaire wrote in *Correspondances*. For me, this meant that the garden's scents, colors, and sounds became a narrative in my blood. The fountain splash singing me to sleep was transmuted into a fragrance I could smell; the shading of the foliage and the accents of the flowers were echoes in my dreaming ear. And all these perfumes, tones, and harmonies were also phrases blossoming in my brain.

There was nothing mystical in this, no hazy sense of "otherness." My symbiosis with the garden, the daily nurturing and tender care, and my bedtime travels through its body were emotional facts as real to me as the pulse in my veins. My garden resonated with my inner life as my mind, charged with passionate memory, drew upon its deep green power.

§

The tenderness and affection I lavished upon my garden was rewarded in many ways. In the spring came a pair of black-chinned hummingbirds, rare woodland visitors seldom seen in cities, who nested in the Oregon grape I planted in a container near the fish fountain.

The greedy fledglings, fuzz balls no bigger than thumbnails, squeaked incessantly as their mother zoomed about the garden gathering pollen. The violet-throated male threatened marauding cats with his needle beak, and even buzzed me when I came too close. As the mahonia unfolded its ruddy new leaves, put out its yellow flower plumes and black grapelike berries, the hummingbird nest among the spiky leaves was stretched to accommodate the growing young birds. Then one day the nest, made of plant fibers, was empty and the family was gone.

Not long after that a red-tailed hawk took to perching on the telephone pole behind the guest house. For minutes at a time the arrogant, hook-beaked bird scrutinized the sea of greenery below for prey; then it spread its broad, dark-tipped wings and floated away, shrieking like a banshee.

With the coming of spring, the garden was constantly crowded with birds. A northern flicker took to drumming on the telephone pole favored by the hawk, punctuating its woodpecker attack with staccato screams. Robins flitted through the branches and splashed in the fountains, bushtits filled the garden with their soft cheepings, towhees trilled in the dense avocado foliage, and a pair of yellow orioles fluted among the honeysuckle. Every so often a cackling crowd of wild parakeets settled on the floss silk tree and noisily made their presence known.

A courting pair of spotted doves took over the deck trellis top. There the puffed-up male shuffled foolishly, ducking his head and making moans while his pretty mate disdainfully stepped away from his attentions and pretended to gaze off into the distance.

Another time I watched a jay trying to spear a fluttering moth through a closed window. The jay jabbed at the glass while the moth, drawn to the light beyond the window, tried to escape this terrifying presence by banging into the pane. Both the bird and the insect, baffled by the transparent barrier between them, were provoked into a frenzy that went on for over an hour before the jay gave up.

One morning, stepping out of my office door, I became aware of a giant presence hovering just above my head. A huge wood stork was perched on my trellis, its four-foot-wide wings spread to catch the sun. The sheer size of the stork dwarfed all the other birds I'd seen in my garden. It was like a visitor from another dimension as its presence seemed to darken the sky and diminish the scale of the place. I was relieved when the big bird flapped its cumbersome wings and took off into the trees.

Other garden visitors were even less welcome. Once I came face-to-face with a foraging raccoon bearing in its jaws the bloody corpse of a neighbor's pet rabbit. Its masked, robber's eyes glared at me from a low avocado branch with such ferocity I turned and ran. Another time a raccoon as big as a small bear charged me in the middle of the night when I went out, naked and half asleep, to investigate a wild yowling. Again I retreated.

After the heavy rains in the winter of 1991–92 flooded the Sepulveda Basin and turned many Malibu canyons into mud rivers, my garden was invaded by an army of earthworms. Following five years of drought, our native worms wriggled to the surface in droves to soak up the rare moisture. In hundreds they chewed the rotting leaves blown down by the storms and passed the mixture of foliage and mud through their bodies, aerating the soil. Walking through the garden, I had to be careful not to squash writhing carpets of the creatures with my boots.

The collapse of a young cabbage tree, snapped in half by the sheer weight of rain on its loose limbs and heavy leaves, was like a kick in the stomach to me. Its stump was a mute reproach for my dereliction in not providing the skinny trunk with enough support.

After the storms, the eucalyptus in the front yard worried me particularly. It had grown too fast, shooting up to twenty feet in height in less than three years, so that the slim trunk was bending under the weight of its branches. In the bursts of sunlight that interrupted the clouds, the wind-tossed eucalyptus discs flashed bright signals of distress. To save the trunk from snapping, I ran out with a ladder in the midst of one of the worst January tempests and sawed several yards off the tree's top.

The rains also brought out a host of long-legged marbled cellar spiders. The spiders tangled up the shrubbery with multiple, domed webs messy with trapped flies and mosquito corpses. Every time

I walked through the garden I was draped with spider streamers, like old Miss Havisham's wedding cake in *Great Expectations*.

❦

My new novel was going well. Working on a computer I had recently acquired to replace my creaking old Selectric, I watched the text inch across the screen with the slow certainty of sap pushing through a tree trunk. This time the story was set in southern California, so the landscape in my head and the one I saw out my office window were not so far apart.

To earn a living, I began to work as a freelance architecture critic for the *Los Angeles Times* and several national design publications. But every moment of my free time, aside from work on the novel, was spent toiling in the yard.

One morning in summer, after weeks of hard work writing and gardening, I had an urge to get up out of the city's web, to go up high and look down on Los Angeles, get a fresh sense of the city as a macrocosm containing the microcosm of my place.

I drove up to Griffith Park, near the Observatory. From this height you're offered a rare overall view of the city. The early fall day was crisp and free of smog, the sky was white with sun, and the silhouettes of the mountains behind me were sharp.

Directly below, Western Avenue scratched a chalk line across the bowl of the Los Angeles Basin all the way to the distant Palos Verdes peninsula and the harbor at San Pedro on the Pacific. At right angles to Western Avenue, Wilshire Boulevard was a spiny, fifteen-mile-long dinosaur with its horned head in the downtown high-rises and its tail dipped in Santa Monica Bay.

Somewhere along that spine was the dot of my garden. That dot might be nothing but a blip on that vast urban screen, but it was the focal point of my personal "mind-map" of Los Angeles. Everyone who lives in L.A. creates his own mind-map; such personal mental charts are the only way to make any sense of the city's sprawl.

Each Angeleno's mind-map has two kinds of topography, physical and emotional, and no two are alike. My physical mind-map centers on my house and garden. From there I trace connections through the lines of streets and network of freeways with the newspaper offices downtown, the universities in Westwood and Exposition Park, Hollywood Boulevard and the Venice boardwalk, the Santa Monica promenade, the Malibu Pier, and Mulholland Drive along the crest of the Hollywood Hills. Beyond these major connections are isolated outposts, including the San Pedro Harbor, Brooklyn Avenue on the Latino east side, Ventura Boulevard in the Valley, Topanga Canyon, the Naples area of Long Beach, and Watts.

In the realm of emotional geography, my mental chart of L.A. has two poles: the Watts Towers and Death Valley.

The Watts Towers are an act of visionary architecture created by Sabatino "Sam" Rodia, an uneducated Italian immigrant, in the flatlands at the bottom of the Los Angeles Basin. For me, the Towers are an icon of imaginative self-invention symbolizing a crucial quality of Los Angeles.

Rodia fashioned a miniature walled city he called *Nuestro Pueblo* ("Our Town"), over a thirty-year stretch from the 1920s to the 1950s. Nuestro Pueblo echoes the church spires, tiled fountains, sunstruck squares, and winding alleyways of Rodia's native Campania.

Working alone, with simple tools and his bare hands, this intuitive genius erected a series of miniature piazzas among an array of skeletal concrete gazebos, pavilions, fonts, and towers—one of the towers is almost a hundred feet tall. He decorated these structures with tile fragments and bottle bottoms, seashells, shards of pottery, and broken teapot spouts; with the imprint of corncobs and faucet tops pressed into cement, and with items rescued from the trash, including a bowling ball and a cowboy boot.

Rodia was a stocky little guy with grizzled cheeks and unwashed Popeye arms sprinkled with glass dust from the blue Milk of Magnesia and green Seven-Up bottles he smashed to decorate his spires. He was a washout as a husband, father, and lover. He abandoned his wife and young sons, failed to sustain relationships with at least two subsequent female companions, and ended up alone for the last forty years of his life—a solitary Italian in a district populated by African-Americans. He was a lonely, obsessed, and gifted man, baffled in his attempts to connect personally with other human beings.

Yet, Rodia turned his life around by the force of his imagination and by taking advantage of that freedom to reinvent oneself that L.A. grants so many of its citizens. His Towers stand for the power of the imagination to recreate the world out of the raw material of memory and yearning.

I got to know the Towers intimately not long after I came to Los Angeles. In the spring of 1985, less than a year after I arrived, I became involved in a campaign to raise money to continue the restoration of the Towers.

In April, the *Herald-Examiner* ran a four-part series I wrote about Rodia's masterpiece. In June 1985 we organized the International Forum for the Future of Rodia's Towers in Watts at the University of Southern California. The Forum attracted a mixture of prominent architects, local officials, and Watts activists. In October, the City of Los Angeles finally came through with a large grant, and the immediate future of the Towers was assured.

When I was researching the newspaper series, I found that the memory of the 1965 riots, or "rebellion," was still very much alive in the minds of the people of Watts, especially among the African-American residents in an area that has since become ethnically mixed with an influx of Latino families.

In that disturbance, one of many such violent urban upheavals in the 1960s, blacks burned down their own community, reducing 103rd Street in the heart of Watts to what came to be known as "Charcoal Alley." Stores were looted and cars torched by rampaging mobs shouting "Kill Whitey!" Thousands of police and National Guardsmen erected barricades to control the nightmare of those six hot August days and nights that cost thirty-four lives and $40 million in property damage.

The events of 1965 remained a shadow haunting the Towers, a dark memory hovering over the present and the future. Social conditions had not improved in the twenty years since the riots, and the natural buoyancy of the people of Watts was undercut by a sardonic stoicism. One young gang member told me, "This here's a jungle and there ain't no Tarzans."

The basic stoicism of South-Central Los Angeles has been periodically blasted by violence. The McCone Commission, appointed by Governor Edmund "Pat" Brown to investigate the causes of the riots, put its finger on the true condition: "When the rioting came to Los Angeles it was not a race riot in the usual sense. What happened was an explosion—a formless, quite senseless, all but hopeless violent protest engaged in by a few but bringing disaster to all." Twenty-seven years later, in April 1992, once again an outraged sense of injustice would erupt in one of the worst outbreaks of violence in American urban history.

In the midst of this urban desolation Rodia's Towers remain a beacon of hope, an emblem of one artist's power to dream his way out of despair.

Death Valley, the other marker in my L.A. mind-map, presents a stark contrast with the Towers. Death Valley's splendid desolation represents for me the fact of the desert surrounding and underlying the willful human habitation of southern California.

Standing on the edge of Dante's View, thousands of feet above Death Valley's floor, you can look so far into the distance you seem to glimpse the beginning of time. Seated on the lip of a waterfall of space, you listen to the beating of your heart in a vibrant silence echoing from the era before the first word was ever spoken.

The colors here are harsh, vivid, and primal: jagged rust red rocks, white salt pans glittering in the brittle sunlight or blackened by a moonless night, a vibrant cobalt blue sky streaked with sullen clouds. The peaks of the Panamint Range across the valley are reflected in saltpan mirrors on the plain below. A desert wind, dry and sweet, ruffles the skin. Night-hawks, small black darts, shriek in the air. Here you're poised on the edge of Creation, suspended between majesty and annihilation.

This is no place for fools. Some who have tried to hike across the Valley floor have been fried by the sun until the fat broiled from their bones and their muscles dried into human jerky. In the high summer of 1991 one experienced hiker was found dead half a mile from the brackish pool of Badwater. The hiker was discovered stretched out on his back as if in sleep, his skin blackened, his flesh shriveled. At 279 feet below sea level, Badwater is one of the hottest places on earth; its ambient air temperatures can climb above 130 degrees Fahrenheit. In the last few frames of a videotape made with his camcorder, the doomed hiker said, "Indeed, this is the real world. One false move and you're dead."

Between these polarities—between the supreme act of imaginative self-invention of Rodia's Towers and the superb hostility of Death Valley that no act of human imagination could ever subsume—stretches my personal Los Angeles, centered on my private Paradise.

9

Tumult and Tranquillity

It's no wonder that our notion of Paradise is rooted in the concept of a garden. The word itself derives from the ancient Persian term *pairi-daeza*, meaning a park or garden, usually enclosed. In the second century A.D. the Carthaginian theologian Tertullian, among others, turned the Greek notion of *paradeisos*—a pleasure garden—into a metaphor for Eden. In Hebrew, the word *eden* means "delight," and *Gan Eden* was a Garden of Delight, rendered by the Latin of the Christian Vulgate as *paradisus voluptatis*. To achieve Paradise was to return to a realm of primal delight.

In the Islamic tradition, however, the Koranic *jannat 'adn*, the "gardens of perpetual bliss," exist only in the sphere of heaven. Eden and Paradise are one heavenly realm in which running waters flow through blissful gardens where the blessed recline at leisure beside their chosen mates. "When God created *jannat 'adn*," an Islamic sage wrote, "He created in it that which the eye had never seen before, that which the ear had never heard before, and that which had never been desired before by any human heart."

The Talmud and the Kaballah, however, speak of two Gardens of Eden, one on earth, the other in heaven. The terrestrial garden is fertile and luxuriant, sensual and passionate; the celestial garden is the paradise of souls. As above, so below: the Garden of Earthly Delight mirrors the landscape of Paradise. "*Gan Eden* and heaven were created by one Word," declares one Talmudic text, "and the chambers of the *Gan Eden* are constructed as those of heaven."

The apocryphal Armenian Gnostic *Book of Adam* describes a moving Edenic scene. The serpent handles Eve roughly, shoving her back up against the trunk of the Tree of Knowledge, threatening her with death if she doesn't eat the offered fruit. Afraid that if she refuses she'll die and that Adam will take a new wife, she agrees to share the fruit with her mate. "We shall die together," she tells herself, "but if not, we shall live together."

At first, Adam tries to resist his wife's temptation; but in the end, he succumbs. "Eve, I would rather die than outlive you," Adam says, and takes the fateful fig. According to the Gnostics, Adam and Eve were the first living creatures ever to perform the act of love. One thinks of William Blake and his wife

Catherine, cavorting naked as Adam and Eve in their London garden. The visionary poet was, Catherine said, "always in Paradise."

In the central panel of Hieronymus Bosch's triptych, *The Garden of Earthly Delights*, a pair of naked lovers floats serenely in a private bubble in the world before the Flood. The woman has her hand on her mate's knee in a gesture both solicitous and erotic. The man strokes her bare belly while gazing lovingly into her eyes.

The world surrounding the couple's bubble is tumultuous. A huge owl looks on while giant red-crested birds and randy goats consort with human revelers more concerned with lust than love. Fantastical architectures crowd the horizon while mounted warriors charge across the plain. Just beneath the lovers' bubble, a solemn face peering out of a porthole confronts an approaching rat.

Eve's body, dazzling as a sheet of light, became a metaphor for the seductive glories of Eden itself in the romantic poetry of medieval Islam. The conceit of garden-as-woman shines through an inscription in the Alhambra. In the Hall of the Two Sisters, a side pavilion opening off the Court of the Lions, is a verse composed by Ibn Zamrak, court poet to Sultan Muhammad V:

I am the garden appearing every morning with
adorned beauty; contemplate my beauty and you
    will be
penetrated with understanding.
How many joyful solaces for the eyes are to be
found in it; in it even the dreamer will renew the
objects of his desire!

The early seventeenth-century English poet
Thomas Campion penned a similar metaphor in his
Fourth Book of Airs:

> There is a garden in her face
> Where roses and white lilies grow;
> A heavenly paradise in that place
> Wherein all pleasant fruits do flow.

The vision of Paradise as a garden is not limited
to the Western and Middle Eastern traditions. In the
Mexican myth of Tlalocan, Paradise is an orchard
rich in fruit trees and flowers watered, like Eden, by
a river. The river issues from the mouth of the god
Tlaloc in his manifestation as a divine toad.

The Tlalocan myth differs from Persian and Hebrew paradise mythology in one major respect: the
Mexican Paradise was first ruled by an Eve-figure

150

alone, by Tlaloc's sister-wife, Chalcioluthlicue. This wise and generous Eve later shared her dominion with her brother-husband, establishing the balance between the male and the female principles vital to the harmony of the natural order.

&

However superb or secure our private Edens may seem, they are always under threat, as I, along with many other Angelenos, discovered in the host of natural and unnatural shocks that struck the city in 1992.

Nineteen ninety-two was a tumultuous year altogether in southern California. In February heavy rains generated massive flooding and mud slides in the Valley and the canyons. In June an earthquake measuring 7.6 on the Richter scale shook and split the ground in the Landers area in San Bernardino County east of the city, and rocked our house as well. In October the Texaco refinery in Wilmington exploded in a ball of flame, smashing windows for miles around and sending a black cloud high in the air.

But these calamities paled beside the April riots, which set many parts of the city burning, destroyed 1,100 buildings, and took more than fifty lives.

151

During the riots Los Angeles was under a dusk-to-dawn curfew for three days. The sirens of ambulances, police cars, and fire trucks screamed ceaselessly while the city tore itself apart, as if trying to release some alien monster from its innards.

The rioting approached our neighborhood boundaries. A minimall and several video stores were looted and burned on Sunset and La Brea boulevards, half a mile away. Ash from the arson fires fell on my plants and the smell of smoke soured the air.

I felt the threat as a wave of chaos smashing against my walls. In my imagination I saw a mob of looters racing down Genesee, brandishing fiery torches, screaming for destruction. For a wild moment I believed that, if I'd possessed a gun, I would have shot anyone who menaced my garden. As it was, I placed a thick, clublike avocado branch beside the back gate, ready to use in defense of my enclave against the madness of the moment.

Washing the ash from my leaves, I cocked an ear for any sound of approaching attack as the sirens continued their shrieking and police helicopters frantically chopped the air. The police and city authorities seemed to flounder, and I felt that only the stoutness of my green walls stood between me and the orgy of rampant violence ruling the streets.

But we were spared. The looters targeted stores, not houses. In a wild free shopping spree, they carried off anything they could lay their hands on, from disposable diapers to wide-screen TVs. As in the Watts riots of 1965, the arsonists mostly torched their own neighborhoods, like flagellants punishing their flesh for the sins of the world. After a few days I set aside my improvised club and unlocked my garden gate.

The riots reminded me once again of the need to be alert wherever I am. Alert in the streets, alert on the roads; sharp even in one's own garden, where a stick in the eye, a thorn in the thumb, a wasp sting in the neck is always a threat for the somnolent.

After the riots subsided, I drove through Koreatown and South-Central to witness the devastation.

Los Angeles looked as if it had been punched in the face by a giant fist. Burned blocks, ugly as broken teeth in the city's mouth, bordered sidewalks bleeding with gummy debris still wet from the firemen's hoses. People on the street, their eyes bruised with shock, seemed stunned by the blows of fate.

Rodia's Towers rode out the storm undamaged, as they had survived the Watts riots of 1965 (which occurred a month after his death in northern California). Even in the throes of anger, the people of

South-Central Los Angeles continued to respect Rodia's *Nuestro Pueblo*, at least enough to leave it alone. Perhaps the Towers remained a symbol of hope amidst despair, a reminder of what a bold spirit might achieve against great odds.

I walked through the Towers once again, and felt the presence of their maker. Sitting in a corner of the Towers, I tried to imagine what Rodia might have felt about the events of April 1992. I don't think he would have been surprised at the recent rage in the streets. The old man had often ranted on about the world going to hell in a handbasket. As an unregenerate anarchist in the Italian tradition, Rodia believed it was always the poor who had to pay for society's sins.

As much as anything else, *Nuestro Pueblo* was an act against the city. Rodia began by marking out his boundaries, constructing the triangular wall that defended his territory. It was only within these safe borders that the idiosyncratic artist felt secure enough to let his imagination flower.

The Towers reminded me that in the tumult of the contemporary world, such intensely personal endeavors counter the darkness of our collective ferocities, and may delay the eternal damnation the human race seems so eagerly to seek.

154

That impulse toward damnation can only be redeemed by an active cultivation of the spirit. For me, such cultivation happens in my garden; in the weeks following the riots I rediscovered how crucial this good green place is to my survival. Like me, it's a living thing requiring constant care to sustain and order its redemptive powers.

If I neglect my garden for more than a day or two, I see the forces of entropy at work: wilting leaves sap many a plant's strength, and the unchecked morning glory strangles the trumpet vine; I find bushes deprived of sunlight by their overgrown neighbors, shrubs wilting for lack of water, and fountains clogged by algae. I see the residue of snails and slugs and the stifling webs of spiders, plants that need nursing to help them back to health, and others that have yet to root themselves firmly.

Apart from the constant need to remedy such consequences of neglect, the garden demands a steady source of tenderness and tending all year round. I'm happy to spend every daylight hour between writing my novel and my journalistic assignments at this activity, even if it means rising every morning before the sun is up.

In the summer heat, especially in September and October, after many dry months, I water my begonias, my chenille plant, and my moisture-loving monsteras, clematis, and freesias every day or they'll wilt in the parched air. If I fail in my duty, these plants soon remind me with sagging stems and crumpled leaves, reproachful as unfed children.

In the fall I cut back overgrown vines and shrubs and weed out the failures. The bougainvilleas, Cape honeysuckle, lavender starflower, jasmines, and solanums have to be thinned in order to bring light and air into their midst and allow for new growth in the spring. I saw away some of the trunks of the over-vigorous banana tree to keep it in control; I prune the orange and lemon trees to concentrate their fruit-bearing branches. I leave the paths unswept because I like the primal-forest crunch of dried autumnal leaves underfoot.

During the wild winter storms I huddle indoors, sensing the rush and power of the wind, watching my young trees bend and sway, anxious that they are properly fastened, nervous they might snap their fragile tops or slip the lines I've fixed to their slender, vulnerable trunks. I witness golden leaves whipped from the liquidambar, purple leaves scattered from the flowering plum, and see the fan palms lashing their fronds.

In early spring, when all the vegetation sprouts, my task is to see that the plants are properly fertilized and fed, that the azaleas and gardenias have their acidic mix, the wisteria its nitrogens and chlorosis-fighting iron chelates, and the greedy clematis its ample nutrients. I turn over waterlogged soil around abutilon and hibiscus roots and scatter the ground nearby with long-term food pellets. I root-feed the flowering prune and plum trees, and also the Hong Kong orchid tree.

All this hectic feeding gives me great pleasure and gratifies my need to nurture. I have to be careful not to enjoy this too much, not to become a hovering mother overnourishing her kids. Some plants can die from too rich a diet, as several of mine did in the first years.

The rhythm of the seasons emphasizes my constant search in the garden's texture for a balance between shade and sun, transparency and opacity, density and clarity. The pulse is never static: The need for shade rules the summer textures, the need for sun governs in winter, and spring and fall are transitions from one to the other.

On hot afternoons in August the thick growth of bougainvillea, jasmine, and abutilon on the overhead trellises keeps the spaces underneath ten or more degrees cooler than the surrounding air. In midwinter the thinned-out foliage lets the sun's light through to warm my face.

&

There's a daily ritual I follow now to keep alert and revive my spirit. Every morning at sunrise I wander through my garden to rediscover my home ground, following Ezra Pound's advice to "Learn of the green world what can be thy place / In scaled invention or true artistry."

Opening my green novel, I pass through bushy lips of night-blooming jessamine, lavender starflower, and coral honeysuckle. These shrubs and vines crowd the steps that open off the rear deck, under a fringe of morning glory and purple-flowered solanum. The dawn is just lighting up the edge of the Hollywood sky, but the greenery I penetrate is still dark.

Immediately, rich scents prickle my nostrils and set the small hairs tingling on my nape. The lingering sweetness of the jessamine, which perfumed the evening with the odors of the Arabian Nights, is cut by the raunchy musk of angel's trumpet and the musty odor of a rockrose bush watered by the splashing of a nearby fountain. These fragrances are carried upon the mulchy smells of the earth waking up to the day, fused with the crisp, cold effusion of the leaves.

The leaves make me shiver as I brush by. The dew on their surface licks my bare arms with cool tongues, marking my passage from outside to inside, from light to dark, intensifying the sensation of entry.

The beat of water spouting from the stone dolphin at the first fountain distracts me from my shivering. I halt beside the water barrel and watch the dolphin's thin stream catch the glance of the brightening sun.

My heart is hammering for reasons I can't define. There are goosebumps on my skin as I tune my ear to the garden's intimate resonances. I know this place so well, yet it always startles me with its fresh nuances of shade and light, its fugue of smells sharp and sweet, its range of textures rough and smooth, its melody of sounds delicate and dangerous.

Above all there are the water noises—whispering, hissing, chuckling, splashing, pounding—that permeate the air like scents turned into sound. Their harmonies counterpoint soft lutes and flutes with the distant hard hoot of a trumpet and the rough rattle of a drum. The sounds carry a subtle warning, an undertone of menace. Dionysus, god of ecstasy, was always accompanied by flute-playing Furies who enjoyed tearing revelers limb from limb in an erotic frenzy.

Yes, there's danger in my garden, and common acts of death. Above the fountain a spider wraps a paralyzed wasp in a small package that looks ready for mailing. The intricate beauty of the web, backlit by the rising sunlight, is a silken pictograph that spells "killing." A parade of tiny Argentine ants carries off a beetle corpse, a hummingbird at the dolphin's mouth drinks through a needle beak that could put my eye out in a flash.

And there are toxins here, lurking in the seeds and pretty flowers of the angel's trumpet, in the milky sap of the crown-of-thorns bush and the pencil tree. There's also the lingering, sickly-sweet stench of a rotting squirrel's corpse I recently removed from under the deck.

The tunnel that beckons me beyond the dolphin fountain is mottled with soft yellow light. The green tube is sheathed in muscular bougainvillea wrapped around the delicate veins of an abutilon vine hung with tiny orange lanterns shivering in the slight dawn breeze. Threaded through them both are the tendrils of a clematis dotted with rosy-nippled blooms, and the wiry filaments of a yellow jasmine. The jasmine's scented, butter-colored flowers flavor the darkness.

A far exit beckons me down the tunnel's length, lit by an angled beam of sun. Vines clutch at me as I push toward the arch of light. Bougainvillea thorns leave tiny scratches on my cheeks and hands. A low-lying abutilon tangle catches in my hair. A jasmine flower hits me in the eye, blinding me for an instant. The exit frames the red clay pot shaped like a miniature Mexican burro and its glowing green sago palm. The image is affectionate and reassuring in this *selva oscura* I must negotiate before I can enter the garden's calm and joyful heart.

Along the way I encounter a marvelous obscenity. The banana palm has put out several hanging purple fruit pods heavy as engorged penises. The pods are splitting, ejaculating a cluster of sticky yellow flowers. When I touch the pods they dribble a thick ichor that coats my fingers with a pungent stink of overripe banana.

The smell is so strong and crude it turns my stomach. The purple banana pod seems to belong to a bull in rut; its stink could be the hot breath of a beast in heat. Gripped by the potent odor, I rest for a moment and lean against one of the redwood posts that support the canopy of vines above.

Then, in the blink of an eye, I see my own burial.

I see myself planted in the warm soil of my garden, wrapped in a shroud of giant banana leaves. Yet, lying in my grave, I feel more alive than ever.

The earth is active around me, dense with roots pushing through the ground, busy with earthworms chewing up rich grains of black clay, thick with nutrients to feed the foliage pushing toward the light above my buried body. Through the porous membrane of the banana skins I feel the earth's good energies and understand why the Russian poet Alexander Kutzenov put his poems in glass preserving jars and buried them at night in his garden. The poet wasn't only secreting his verses from Stalin's reign of terror; he was also, I imagine, hoping to infuse them with the power of the dark and dreaming soil.

Startled from thoughts of burial by the swift shadow of a hummingbird flitting through the shade, I step away from the banana pods and stroll on, to where Gertie, the painted plywood yard cow, a black and white Holstein, dances lightly on the keyboard of an old harmonium I found abandoned in the garden shed.

162

I have only the miniature organ's keyboard, but Gertie makes ghostly music tripping her hooves on the black and white keys. Her silent tune is counterpointed by the tinkling of copper wind chimes and the gentle clatter of the Greek sheep bells and small Buddhist temple bells I've suspended on chains from the upended wrought-iron chandelier fixed to the crown of the wooden totem pole.

And then I'm at the center of this private Eden, standing in the midst of a bright clearing. Here blood red bougainvillea bracts rub against the royal purple of princess flowers. A cobalt blue clematis vine climbs a trellis above a miniature fig tree. Daylilies push forth languorous yellow and velvet carmine blooms on long-necked stalks. Two abutilon bushes, grown into trees, are laden with orange-veined flowers. A trumpet vine, framing an archway, droops pale violet blossoms onto papery scarlet pomegranate flowers.

Three fountains add lively notes to serenade such splendor. One burbles above the naked cherub, overflowing a dish that spills water down his plump belly. The leaping fish puts out a bolder trumpeting sound. A third, its layered levels topped by a terra-cotta swan, gives off a gentle tinkle. Papyrus stalks, fifteen feet tall, shoot up into the sky above the water, sturdy as the columns at the temple of Luxor. I dip my fingertips in the cold fountain water and touch them to my eyes to refresh my sight.

The bright arena is charged with the coarse, musky odor of ripe fig, which, according to Hebrew legend, was the fruit that the serpent offered Eve and Adam in the original Garden. These fruits dangle like plump purple scrotums. The fig's intensely sexual smell lies over the earthy aroma of rosemary and the fragrances of orange blossom, gardenia, lavender, and osmanthus.

If I stand very still here, in the buttery green-gold light of early morning, other creatures gather. A mockingbird settles in the jessamine to pluck the ripe white berries while making loud kissing sounds, like a mother planting a smackeroo on her baby's cheek. A scrub jay perches on the cherub fountain dish and spreads its tail in the cool water, pausing to release a raucous yawp. A pair of spotted doves cuddle in a corner, heads together, cooing intimately to one another. A flock of bushtits fills the air with twitterings and a bumblebee buries its face in a purple princess flower, bending the bloom's neck with its greedy weight.

A female possum stares at me from her hiding place in the trumpet vine, regarding me with ancient, myopic eyes, sniffing me out with her wet pink snout. The possum's smooth and timid face contrasts oddly with her scruffy, ratlike body and tail. From the wariness of her expression I suspect the possum has babies clinging to the teats hidden in her belly pouch.

Then there's the multitude of insects. Swallowtail butterflies and painted ladies mingle with bees, wasps, hornets, midges, mites, spiders, ladybugs, crickets, and those perky grasshoppers James Joyce called "Gracehopers" for their habit of clasping their front legs together as if in prayer: "The Gracehoper was always jigging ajog, hoppy on akkant of his joyicity."

This isn't the end of the insect realm's joyicity. Earwigs crowd under stones and munch their way through rotting logs. Ants sup on aphid honeydew. Cutworms hide in the ground by day, curled up in sleep, to emerge at night to feast on young plants. These larvae become the night-flying moths that crowd the garden lights.

Listening to the drowsy bees sucking pollen, I'm reminded of a marvelous analogy between making a poem and making a beehive offered by the Russian poet Osip Mandelstam.

In his essay "A Conversation About Dante," Mandelstam conjured up the image of a host of bees, "endowed with the brilliant stereometric instinct," to describe the structural pattern of the *terza rima* Dante used in *The Divine Comedy*. Like the bees, Mandelstam wrote, Dante constructed his complex, multi-faceted word-hive from within, so that "space virtually emerges out of itself."

A cleavage in the wall of greenery at my back opens into an enclosure dim and dank, a tropical chamber haunted by shadows. It's still and silent but for the trickle of the garden's last fountain hidden in a corner. Beyond, at the back fence of my garden, is a red and white street sign I salvaged that commands STOP.

To enter here, I must pass my private totem pole capped by its stone owl, sacred to Pallas Athena, virgin of the flashing eyes, goddess of the Parthenon, protector of agriculture and the civilized arts. Below the owl is the Aesculapian snake, "soother of cruel pangs, a joy to men," and the small white Buddha, his smiling face eager for the rising sun. Above the Buddha is a small clay bowl filled with a votive offering of my hair clippings. A scrub jay perches there, grooming himself like a prom beau fussing with his blue tuxedo.

Overnight a spider has built an elaborate pattern of concentric, radiating circles linking the totem pole to the portal. The filaments cover my face like a bridal veil as I push on. In its toils I feel momentarily blinded, panicked by that sticky, delicate clutch.

I break through into a chamber roofed with honeysuckle and bougainvillea, bounded by a wall of morning glory. Large-leaved plants circling the fountain undulate in the morning's gentle zephyr. The floss silk tree lifts its olive green trunk through the overhead laths and spreads a parasol of pink flowers to shelter me from the sky's increasing glare. The dappling of the light through this dense canopy recalls Gerard Manley Hopkins's "Pied Beauty," in which "All things counter, original, spare, strange," resonate with sensations "swift, slow; sweet, sour; adazzle, dim."

Resting on the bench under the lemon tree, I pluck a yellow fruit and breathe in its tart, spermy scent. A deep sense of peace floods me as I loll back on the bench and look up through the cathedral vault formed by the lattice of Cape honeysuckle stems. Golden green light seeps through the leaves, striking small flames from the orange flowers. A young mockingbird, throat swollen with song, trills and crackles in the bright morning air.

The dynamic equilibrium between clarity and density, growth and decay, memory and experience, metaphor and fact, humanity and nature manifested in this good green book I've written on the earth has seeped deep into my bones. It has smoothed out my short-term mood swings, provided me with a longer breath, soothed me in a new intimacy with the cyclical life of the natural sphere. This gained sense of balance helps me ride out those bumps in my life that used to trip me up and make me feel lost.

In these ways my garden has made me even as I've made it. It has connected my head with my hands and rooted both sensibilities in a shared ground, cultivating a quietness I never knew could flourish in the agitated soil of my temperament. Making my garden has taught me that delight and despair move through the seasons of one's life in a constant round of renewal.

Yes, this garden is my own true Paradise, carrying a personal echo of Eden as Adam experienced it on the sixth day of Creation, when God gave him the power to name every living thing on the newly-made planet called Earth. It has the form of that imagined Eve who comes toward me now, naked in the morning air. Her flesh gives off a female heat, drawn from the sunshine filtering through the leafy canopy above, and the smell of her warm body nourishes my heart.

About the Author

Architect and novelist Leon Whiteson was born in Zimbabwe and has lived in England, Spain, Greece, and Canada. He has published several novels in England and Canada and four books on architecture, as well as articles for magazines. He now lives in Hollywood with his wife, Aviva, and writes fiction and architecture criticism for the *Los Angeles Times*, in between tending his garden.